ROCKET
YOUR
POTENTIAL

My 2022

Clair,

To you unlimited
potential!

Enjoy the journey!!

Best,

Phil

ROCKET YOUR POTENTIAL

A Career Handbook for
Rising Stars & Future Women Leaders

PHYLLIS EHRLICH

gatekeeper press
Columbus, Ohio

ROCKET YOUR POTENTIAL:

A Career Handbook for Rising Stars & Future Women Leaders

Published by **Gatekeeper Press**

2167 Stringtown Rd, Suite 109

Columbus, OH 43123-2989

www.GatekeeperPress.com

Library of Congress Control Number: 2022932698

ISBN (paperback): 9781662924538

eISBN: 9781662924545

To my incredible parents, Laura and Morty,
whose unconditional love and support gave me the confidence
and courage to always reach for the stars.
You live on in my heart forever.

Acknowledgments

Heartfelt thanks to the many wonderful people who have helped guide and inspire me both professionally and personally.

You fuel my passions, encourage me through tough times, and challenge me to be better.

Gratitude to my family and dearest friends for your unwavering love—you ground me when needed and allow me to soar.

Special thanks to Craig and Joel. Collaborating with both of you on this mission has been infinitely rewarding.

Table of Contents

PREFACE   6

INTRODUCTION   7

Section **1**   ASSEMBLE YOUR FLIGHT CREW   15

Develop Your Relationships   16
Assess and Strengthen Your Network   21
Make Self-Awareness a Superpower   29
Find a Role Model, Be a Role Model   39

Section **2**   BLAST OFF   51

Excel by Being Passionately Curious   52
Work Smarter and Harder Than Anyone Else   58
Pay Your Dues   68
Bring a Unique Spark   71
Value Customer Service   78
Ask for Expert Advice   83
Work with Differences   89

NAVIGATE YOUR COURSE   **97**

Section

Be Realistic, Be Resilient, Be Relentless   98
Embrace Change and Hang on Tight   106
Build Consensus from the Top Down and the Bottom Up   112
Manage Your Boss   118
Get a Thumbs-Up for a Heads-Up   125
Manage Hardships and Turbulence   130
Consider Corporate Culture   136
Prepare for Leadership Opportunities   142
Stretch Yourself to Stay Relevant   147

SOAR TO NEW HEIGHTS   **155**

Section

Ace Your Internal Interview   156
Know When It Is Time to Move On   161
Pay it Forward   170
Rocket Your Higher Purpose   176

ENDNOTES   **182**

ABOUT THE AUTHOR   **186**

Preface

I believe that when women rise to powerful positions, they can enrich their lives, shape the success of their companies, and make the world a better place. The last years of college and the first few years of your career are the launch pad for your future success. To rocket means to rise swiftly, spectacularly, and catapult with force. This handbook will help you create your own personal plan to accelerate and elevate every dimension of your professional trajectory. Are you ready to define, fuel, and realize your unlimited potential?

If so, come with me on this journey, where I take my many years of experience and growth and prepare you for the road ahead personally and professionally.

Let's take off!

Phyllis Ehrlich, New York City, 2022

Introduction

You want to talk about not being prepared? My first job out of college was with a family-owned magazine publishing company called American Baby. American Baby created a wide variety of magazines, sampling, couponing programs, and even a cable TV show, all providing valuable information for expectant and new moms. I have always been a hard worker, and I threw myself into the job. There was so much I didn't know about the world of work, but I thought I could figure it out. I figured out high school, I figured out college, I figured out part-time jobs, so how hard could it be?

I soon realized that it could, in fact, be very hard. There are so many rules (almost all of them unwritten) about how to behave, how to manage yourself, and perhaps, most importantly, how to treat other people. I learned this quickly on my first-ever business trip for American Baby. I flew to Chicago with the publisher and co-owner of the company. In Chicago we were joined by our salesperson, Cynthia. From there we drove to Fremont, Michigan, to meet with Gerber, one of our top advertisers.

I was terrified about so many things—what to wear, how to act, and how to interact with clients. Fortunately for me, Cynthia took me under her wing. She even invited me to stay at her beautiful apartment overlooking the Chicago skyline the night before we headed to Fremont. She gave me great background information about the clients we were going to meet with and explained that the culture at Gerber was conservative and reserved. I observed her professional business attire and demeanor, sprinkled with a large dose of warmth. She didn't have to help me prepare for the trip, but she did. We became dear friends and over the years have shared many professional and personal highs and lows with enduring love and respect. For whatever reason she took an interest in me and positioned me to be successful on my first client visit. I was lucky that Cynthia—and so many other women—have provided me with generous support over the course of my career. Back then I remember not knowing how to figure it out or who I could turn to. If it wasn't for them, I don't think I could have just "hard-worked" myself to the place I am today.

I remember wishing that someone had written a handbook to help me navigate my early career hurdles. Looking back, I realized that our careers are made up of a long series of pivotal moments. In those moments I sometimes wished there was someone to turn to who had experienced or seen the same thing I was going through. That is what I have done with this book.

Who Is This Book For?
This book is for a motivated person with a plan. More specifically, it is for women early in their careers who want to build a strong launch pad for themselves. If you're a college senior, new hire, or a rising star, *Rocket Your Potential* can help you accelerate your professional trajectory.

On the other hand, if you are a person who is willing to let her career flow based on whatever way the river takes you, this is probably not the book for you. Ditto if you are not particularly motivated or committed to making a contribution to where you work to build the base for a rewarding and fulfilling career.

There are thousands of books on the market directed toward executives and other senior leaders, but few speak directly to the issues we face in the first stage of our careers. Of those books, even fewer are directed toward the unique challenges of women in the workplace. Over the course of my career, I have seen a pattern with women who believe that the company they work for should establish their career trajectory for them. They believe that the company is like family and will look out for them. This book is intended to help you create your own opportunities by being prepared for those pivotal moments when they occur. And, in the long run, I believe that when women rise into powerful positions, they can make their companies and the world a better place. Since I can't physically be beside you to help you rocket your career journey, I have captured some strategies in this book to help you during those pivotal moments.

How This Book Is Organized

If you wanted to, you could read this book from front to back, and I believe you would learn a lot and enjoy yourself. But as I considered the format, I wanted to create something that was more of a handbook-style resource. With that goal, I wrote each of the chapters to address a specific issue that women face in the early part of their career—or even later. In that sense it serves as a resource at your fingertips that you can refer to as you are experiencing a specific issue. Each chapter is brief and to the point and offers a set of specific recommendations.

Rocket Your Potential is divided into four sections that address specific work themes:

SECTION 1, *Assemble Your Flight Crew*, is all about the importance of the people in your career. We pay particular attention to your network—what it does, how to build it in a genuine and personal way, and who is already a part of it. At the end of the section, I also address the importance of role models and how to find the right ones for you.

In **SECTION 2**, *Blast Off*, I ask you to look inward. We explore the personal resources and mindset that you bring to the table and understand how they are an important part of your career foundation.

SECTION 3, *Navigate Your Course*, is the longest section in the book because it covers the longest arc of your career. In this section, we explore some of the potential landmines as well as opportunities that can pop up.

SECTION 4, *Soar to New Heights,* asks you to consider your higher purpose. How do you stretch yourself to stay relevant, change course if necessary, and begin to pay it forward?

At the end of each chapter, there is a list of the primary takeaways from that chapter called the "Chapter Countdown."

About Me

In many ways, I still see myself as a Brooklyn girl. We were all expected to work, which I did almost as far back as I can remember. As you will read in this book, some of the most formative work experiences in my life were from working in our family business, a neighborhood toy and sporting goods store.

That job, as well as other early work, helped me appreciate the importance of hard work and customer focus that has served me well later in executive roles with the Walt Disney Company, Turner Broadcasting, and Time Warner Cable Media. Currently, I am a group vice president at Spectrum Reach, and there is one thing that ties all my experience together. No matter what company I am with or what my job description is, I think it is my responsibility to remember what it was like getting started, and it is my job to help other women rocket their own careers.

And before you think of this book as "just another leadership book written by a driven woman without a life," I am just as proud (if not prouder) and work just as hard on the other roles in my life as a daughter, mother, stepmother, wife, and friend. In fact, many of my personal challenges and experiences have powered my professional resilience. My work does not define me, but it is important to me that I do the best I can at the highest level I can. And I have learned so much along the way.

About Joel

While I have written this book from my own perspective, many of the examples and stories come from observing events and behaviors of other people, including friends, coworkers, and, most importantly, my husband, Joel. In most chapters there are stories and examples that he provides, which I call "Joel's Take." You will see that Joel and I look at some of these career steps from different perspectives. We think this adds richness to the narrative and demonstrates that there is more than one way to rocket your career. Because he shows up frequently in the book, I want to include a little bit about Joel's professional background to provide you with a bit of context.

Joel is my professional and personal partner, the love of my life, and my soul mate for almost three decades (more on this throughout the book). He is an accomplished sales and marketing executive and entrepreneur with an impressive career at companies including American Baby (where we met), Marvel, and Warner Bros. Joel taught me the basics of sales and marketing. He excels at getting into other people's comfort zones and forming long-lasting relationships. As a former actor and brilliant presenter and public speaker, he gave me the know-how and courage to give a speech to 5,000 dietitians at their annual industry conference. You will see that Joel's unique brand of wisdom, kindness, and charisma help bring these pages to life.

Joel's Take

I wish I could have read a book like this in my twenties. I would have been better prepared for what was to come along the meandering route of my own career journey. I started as a theater major, not truly having a vision of where that would take me. My career stops included jobs as a fourth-grade teacher, pharmaceutical sales representative, advertising sales representative for trade and consumer magazines, sales and marketing representative for major entertainment titans, business owner, and now, college professor. Along the way I have connected with and tried to be helpful to countless young people at the beginning of their careers. That's why I was so excited when Phyllis invited me to contribute to the book by offering my take on some of the topics that she addresses. Phyllis and I share many of the same values and life goals, but boy, are we different. We have different personalities, work styles, and career experiences. You know what they say, opposites attract. What they don't tell you is that opposites can later drive each other crazy unless they share common long-term views and values. And we do. Look at it this way, at one point in our career, Phyllis represented Scooby Doo and I exploited Batman and Superman. Our careers were as different as day and night, but we had one common goal: to succeed in the tasks presented to us—while always giving back.

One value we share is the desire to help others, and we both consider it our higher calling. But, because we have different views, we don't always have the same approach to dealing with the issues that you may face early in your career. We use that to create additional substance for the book by providing another perspective—mine. We hope two perspectives add to the richness of your reading and offer alternative approaches to getting where you want to go. And remember, every comment we make is from real experiences. Enjoy the ride—and the stories!

So many people and leadership programs have helped propel my career in so many ways, and this book is a way for me to give back and pay it forward. Even though I can't be beside you for every step of your career journey, I have compiled some of the critical lessons, tips, and tactics I have learned from experience, trial and error, and generous role models. Looking back and thinking about what got me to where I am today—and what keeps me going strong—there are many key insights. I hope that there are elements of my story that resonate with you. In this book I focus on the skills and tactics that will help you reach your highest potential and achieve your long-term goals, and I have attempted to do so with a unique style, as free of business jargon as possible, and with a sense of humor. So, let's countdown your launch plan so that you can be seen for your talents and relentlessly pursue excellence in all you do. Blast off time is right now!

Chapter Countdown
THE MAIN TAKEAWAYS FROM THIS CHAPTER:

- This book is for a motivated person with a plan—or one who needs a plan. It is organized in the sequence of events in a typical career arc.
- However, the trajectory of your career will be unique to you. But I can help by presenting some of the predictable challenges, benefits, and decisions you may encounter.
- Two heads are better than one, so I also include the perspectives of another successful businessperson, my husband, Joel.
- This book can serve as a handbook. You can read it front to back or you can just read the chapters that you need as you take your career journey.

1

Section

ASSEMBLE YOUR FLIGHT CREW

CHAPTER 1
Develop Your Relationships

———

You might be surprised to see that I am starting this book by talking about, of all things, relationships. You might have expected more of what we see in so many business and leadership books that are out there—conquer the world, face your fears, and take no prisoners!

Instead, I want you to think about the people you most like being with, interacting with, spending time with, and embarking on journeys with. What traits and characteristics do they have? How would you describe them? Warm, caring, generous, patient, interesting, selfless, thoughtful, smart, or maybe they have a sunny, optimistic personality? Do you share similar traits, or are you attracted to them because you appreciate their different attributes? What they probably all have in common is that none of them is perfect. Yet, for some reason you have bonded with them and, as a result, your life is better.

It's All About Relationships
Looking back at my career and what made me most successful, it wasn't just working hard, being creative, or being intelligent. It was—and is—always about the relationships I have been fortunate to have and that I knew were necessary and vital to my success in any endeavor. Whether in our personal or

professional lives, there is very little that endures like fulfilling, long-lasting, meaningful relationships.

What many people forget is that our clients and colleagues are just as human as we are. They may be going through myriad personal challenges in their life, including illness, divorce, kids, parents, financial problems, and career issues. Sometimes we need to look beneath the surface to understand what their lives are all about. It reminds me that we should remember the old familiar axiom, "Don't judge a book by its cover." Don't make assumptions. The more you know—and truly care—about the people you deal with, the better chance there is for a meaningful relationship to flourish. You need to be part detective and part psychologist.

Sometimes People Come Before Business

Many years ago, I had a business lunch with a client who had a reputation of being fair but tough. The day we met she just didn't seem herself. My casual and genuine show of concern developed into a lifelong friendship. She confided in me that she was extremely concerned about her teenage daughter. By asking questions, showing empathy, and even making some suggestions, we created a bond that we could never have made over a business discussion. And, as it turned out, we did not discuss any business that day. But from that day on, she always gave me an extra dose of both fairness and business.

Asking questions at a meeting and surfacing other people's needs and wants—putting them before yours—creates a whole different image of who you are. And, of course, it must be genuine. After all, you can't fake authenticity. People will see right through pretend interest.

Sometimes deepening your relationship with someone is not always about that person directly but how you treat the people who are important to that person. Being helpful to their team, coworkers, and even their family can strengthen that connection. It's important to understand, acknowledge, and embrace those who mean the most.

For example, when I was at Turner Broadcasting, we had a great annual client trip to the Atlanta Braves' spring training. The trip was designed to thank top clients for their advertising business and was a great opportunity to bond with them and, maybe even more importantly, to get to know their families. Along with Joel and our son, Andrew, we invited my big Kellogg's client, Sandy, her husband, Brian, and their daughter, Alex. During that fun weekend, we forged a lifetime bond and friendship. Brian is a law enforcement officer, and we learned about his background and job—quite different than TV advertising. Andrew and Alex swam with the dolphins at Sea World, and to this day, the photos from the trip are a wonderful memory. Although we live in different cities and Sandy left Kellogg's years ago, we keep in touch via social media and cheer on each other's family celebrations and milestones.

Follow the Golden Rule

Do unto others as you would have them do unto you. One mistake people often make is not valuing people who aren't directly important to them at that moment. I believe many people don't even realize they are doing it. From your office building security guard to the summer interns, how you treat everyone you meet matters. Think about each one of those contacts as an opportunity for a touchpoint. One of those interns may be a future vice president of marketing or become someone who steps up to help you with a personal need some day. The administrative assistant you treat with respect is more apt to get you a meeting with his or her high-level boss. Throughout the years, I have always asked my assistants how my coworkers treat her or him. If I hear good things, I am more likely to talk to or meet with that coworker. If they are rude or dismissive to my assistant, it's highly unlikely they will ever get to me. Making these kind of connections feels good and, just as importantly, creates an image of you that is consistent with the traits you look for in other people.

Sometimes It's About a Donut

And sometimes it is about a heartfelt thank you or simple token of appreciation. For example, who doesn't enjoy a donut or home-baked muffin to start off their workday a little sweeter? How easy is it for you to simply give a compliment for a job well done in a team meeting?

How do you maintain and grow relationships?

- Stay in touch via emails and personal notes.
- Connect via social media when appropriate.
- Remember someone's birthday or their child's graduation.
- Provide value—extend invitations and/or share learnings from industry organizations and events to help others be more connected and up to date.
- Go beyond texting—differentiate yourself and pick up the phone and leave a message.

As Michelle Obama pointed out in her memoir, *Becoming*, "Friendships between women, as any woman will tell you, are built of a thousand small kindnesses . . . swapped back and forth and over again."

Joel's Take

One of my career highlights was helping Marvel Comics evolve from a comic book publisher to a leader in the entertainment and consumer products world. As senior vice president, I had the amazing opportunity to show the world that Spider-Man and X-Men could teach nutrition, build self-esteem,

and stimulate the imagination of kids—all while skyrocketing sales for Marvel and key partners. As a result of building successful, ground-breaking partnerships with top brands, including McDonald's, Nabisco, and Kraft Foods, I was named "Youth Marketer of the Year" by *Brandweek* magazine. My highlighted quote in the cover story article was, "It all comes down to relationships." The one thing you take from job to job is your reputation. I was able to capitalize on the strong business relationships I brought to my role at Marvel because people trusted me to deliver and over-deliver on my promises and results. I always care about my clients being successful—and show strong interest in them as people.

Chapter Countdown
MAIN TAKEAWAYS FROM THIS CHAPTER:

- It all comes down to relationships.
- Sometimes people come before business.
- Follow the Golden Rule.
- Stay in touch, and nurture your relationships.
- Small gestures of kindness make a big impact.

CHAPTER 2
Assess and Strengthen Your Network

———————

The old mental image of networking gives a lot of people the creeps—and for good reason. For many of us it conjures up negative images of a bunch of people walking around some hotel convention or seminar, wearing a "Hello, my name is . . ." nametag, carrying a watery drink, and making meaningless conversation in the hope of . . . well, what? In the old networking model, there always seemed to be the unspoken air of "What can you do for me?" behind it all.

Maybe networking is an outdated term that doesn't accurately describe a group of people who help each other. In fact, if you do an internet search today using the term "network," you are most likely to land on an instructional video for setting up your home Wi-Fi. Maybe "support network" comes closer. That, at least, describes a beneficial intent in the term. In my mind networking means creating a mutually supportive group of people. Then, over the course of our lives, we should gradually, and with clear intention, build our network. One of the things you will see in this book is that so many of the good things that have happened to me in my work and in my life are a result of other people who had my best interest in mind. And perhaps, vice versa.

Networking Is Like a Bank Account

At this stage of my career, I spend much more time thinking about how to help the other people in my network than I do about how they can help me. I enjoy helping people if I can, particularly women launching their careers. For one thing, nothing is as rewarding to me as when I can help someone or connect them with someone else who can help them. I have come to think about networking as a kind of bank account—I must make a deposit before I can make a withdrawal, and I have come to love making deposits into my support network account.

Like a bank account, I don't spend frivolously. The balance grows, and I may never need to tap into it—and that's great. But, when and if I need to reach out to someone in my network for help, I have the social capital in place. As you will see throughout this book, at critical junctures in my career, my network has propped me up and come through for me in a big way. You should always be networking throughout your career because you never know what might develop on both a professional and personal level.

You Already Have a Network

In our old model of the networking cocktail party, the idea was to connect with strangers to expand your network. Realize that people you already know are part of your core network. For example, we tend to overlook our own friends and family members as critical participants in our support network. I landed my first paying summer job at age fourteen through a friend of my parents. You may want to reconnect with high school friends who might benefit from staying in touch with you and vice versa. The same goes for college friends or people you met while working in seasonal jobs.

Don't overlook the non-business circles in which you are active. Other places where you connect with people might include:

- Your gym
- Religious organizations
- Parents' groups
- Other professionals and service providers
- Friends of friends and family.

Expand Your Network

Here are some specific ways to expand your network:

First, Joel's Take

Put yourself out there and be warm and friendly. Phyllis and I were flying home to New York City from a business trip Washington, DC. The first come, first served shuttle flight was crowded, and there were very few seats remaining. Only minutes before takeoff, we saw a man, looking stressed and out of breath, rushing down the aisle to find a seat. I stood up, offered him the remaining seat in our row, and helped put his luggage in the overheard compartment. A thank you and conversation ensued, and it turned out that our seatmate was a fascinating and formidable former Assistant US Attorney General. From that day on, Arnie and I developed a close personal and professional relationship. What started as a simple gesture of concern resulted in numerous high-level connections and business ventures for me, including being asked to serve as a Northeast Trustee of the Boys & Girls Club of America.

Attend industry events, trade shows, and conferences, virtually and/or in person. If you are in person and hear an impressive speaker, go up and thank them at the end of the talk. You never know what might happen. One of my favorite networking stories is about an aspiring young marketer named David, who came up to me after I gave a lively presentation at a kids' marketing conference. Just a few years into his career, David handed me his business card and said, "Thank you for an incredibly inspiring talk. Someday I want to work for you—and be like you." I didn't have any opportunities at the time, but David continued to keep in touch. When I went to oversee promotions and licensing at DC Comics/Warner Bros., I had an opportunity that was a good fit for David. David worked for me for many years and has gone on to be a senior theme park executive with an impressive resume of his own.

When you meet people in person, always ask to exchange business cards. If you don't have one, make one to be taken seriously. Companies like Vistaprint offer inexpensive, good quality options. Join industry organizations, which very often have a reduced membership fee for young executives. If you have a passion for a particular cause (e.g., prevention of pet cruelty), get involved with a charitable organization where you may meet like-minded individuals. Make a list of people you admire and send them an email or personal note. Add value by including something that might be of interest to them, including a recent article or white paper. Use the worksheet at the end of the chapter to help you identify all the people you know and how you may ask them to introduce you to their network.

For people you don't know, you need to be creative and courageous. You never know where your next networking opportunity may come from. One of my former mentees was interested in making a career pivot from marketing to content creation. We attended an industry event together, where the speaker was the charismatic head of a cable TV network. She didn't get the opportunity to speak to him at the event but ended up on the NYC subway with him on the way back to their mutual offices. She was brave enough to strike up a conversation but didn't ask if she could reach out to him to schedule an informal conversation for career advice. Knowing this person was a passionate mentor, I recommended she send him an email with a catchy subject line. At the time, *Girl on the Train* was a best-selling book, and I suggested that for her subject line. She sent him a short, compelling email. What was the response? Within twenty minutes, he wrote back and invited her to his office for a meeting. She received some excellent advice and was on her way to developing a plan to change her career course.

Stand out from the pack. When I was an adjunct professor of integrated marketing at New York University's School of Professional Studies graduate program, there were always two or three students in the class who stood out on the first day of class. In some cases, star students stood out with an email introduction even before the first day of the semester. What did these students have in common? Enthusiasm, passion, and a willingness to help me with anything from PowerPoint presentations to technology and social media needs. It was my pleasure to recommend these students for internships and full-time jobs when they graduated. Many of them keep me posted on their career progress and seek advice from time to time.

Subscribe to blogs in your industry or desired areas of interest. Very often you can contact the author directly.

LinkedIn, the 800-Pound Gorilla

As the old riddle goes, "Where does an 800-pound gorilla sleep?" The answer: "Anywhere it wants to." LinkedIn is the 800-pound gorilla of professional networking. It has changed everything, including making it easy to connect with the people already in your network and reconnect with people you have lost touch with. It is also a terrific place to do research on others and determine what you have in common before connecting. The bad news is that, because it is so easy, many people choose quantity over quality, and that's a mistake. Remember the banking analogy. You should be building your network with an eye toward contributing to others as well as making strategic connections for yourself. At some point, hundreds and hundreds of connections go beyond the point of diminishing returns. For the purpose of this chapter, think of it as a vehicle to strengthen your existing network. Just remember to follow good LinkedIn protocol. For anyone looking for a deep dive into LinkedIn, there are many books and courses, as well as plenty of free online videos and articles. In the meantime, here are some tips, tricks, and things I have learned about LinkedIn from practice:

- LinkedIn is THE professional social media platform and tool.
  ....

- Other social media platforms like Facebook, Instagram, Twitter, YouTube, and TikTok need to be carefully curated and ideally kept private. Recruiters look at all social media platforms they can, and this can make or break someone getting a job offer. Beware of inappropriate photos and comments.
  ....

- In many ways LinkedIn has replaced the resume. If you're still in college, craft a professional-looking LinkedIn profile now. It will be crucial when seeking internships.
  ....

- Look at and learn from LinkedIn profiles of people you admire or aspire to be.
  ....

- Have a photographer friend or a professional take your photo.
  ....

- The summary sentence at the top of your profile is the most important text on your page. Say something powerful about your personal brand. Don't waste the space on your current job title.
  ....

- Craft a strong description for the "About" section. Get a friend to proofread it for you.

  ....

- Follow good LinkedIn etiquette. Don't send requests to people randomly, and always write a personal message. Like many other senior-level professionals, I don't accept requests from people I don't know unless they make the effort to add a note telling me why they are reaching out to me.

  ....

- Don't forget LinkedIn's value as a database. Before you meet with someone, review their LinkedIn profile.

  ....

- If you know someone well enough and see someone in their network you'd like to connect with, it's okay to ask.

  ....

- Recommendations and endorsements might be valuable for someone in the early years of their career.

  ....

- Finally, don't underestimate the value of hiring a LinkedIn expert to help you. My latest LinkedIn profile is the result of work I did with a great friend of mine who is a branding expert. When I recently gave a keynote address to a group of rising leaders, the facilitator complimented my profile and asked the attendees to review it as a homework assignment. I'm pretty sure that was the first (and only) time I was a homework assignment!

In summary, remember that you are not starting from scratch. You already have an existing network. What do you need to do to strengthen it? We have included a worksheet at the end of the chapter to help you determine your existing network and identify possible additions.

Chapter Countdown

MAIN TAKEAWAYS FROM THIS CHAPTER:

- Networking is like a bank account—make many deposits and make withdrawals only as needed.
- Identify your existing network.
- Be creative and courageous to expand your network.
- Maximize LinkedIn as your professional networking tool.
- Stand out and be memorable.

Worksheet instructions:

Step 1.

In the inner circle, write the names of individuals you consider already in your personal/professional network.

Step 2.

In the middle circle, write the names of people who you know (even distantly) who you feel you would like to have in your network and be in theirs.

Step 3.

In the outer circle, write the names of people you do not know, but would like to connect with.

People you know but not in your network

People you don't know and not in your network

People in your current network

CHAPTER 3

Make Self-Awareness Your Superpower

I am convinced that sustainable success does not happen without a high degree of self-awareness, whether you are talking about your career or your personal relationships. Your willingness and ability to look openly and honestly at your own strengths and weaknesses will directly impact whether you rocket your potential or remain on the launch pad. I have seen young people as well as seasoned professionals with exceptional skills and enviable drive derail because they were, as their coworkers described them, clueless about how their behavior impacted other people. As a result, they never truly understand how they are perceived by others and are surprised when they are unable to reach their goals.

Joel's Take: Even Superman Needs Feedback

I was an executive at DC Comics/Warner Bros., working out of DC Comics's New York City headquarters. Much of my responsibility was to lead the leveraging of Batman and Superman in licensing and promotions and to prevent others from illegal use of our brands. It was a pretty hefty, high-profile job.

I had to travel quite a bit to the Warner Bros. studios in Burbank, CA, to meet with the licensing group. Imagine a dozen or so people around the table giving financial updates on their superhero characters as well as Looney Tunes characters, Harry Potter, and other Warner Bros. brands. I didn't know these other people very well, so when it was my turn to report, I decided to endear myself to them by being highly exuberant, overly friendly, and dramatic so that they would like me, respect me, and understand the success I was driving.

I eventually became close to a guy from that group named Jordan, who eventually became an executive vice president. We got to know and trust each other and remain close friends to this day. One day we were having coffee and I asked him for some candid feedback: "Jordan, give me a sense of how you view me and maybe what you think I could do better." I was caught off guard by his response when he said, "When I first met you at those meetings at Warner Bros., I really thought you were a phony. You didn't have credibility in my mind. I thought it was just a con job because you didn't come off as sincere." I thought about that for a minute then asked him what I did to make that impression. He said, "You were overly friendly, pushy, braggadocious, and it came off as fake."

Wow. In retrospect, asking for that feedback was one of the most important things I have done in my career. I thanked Jordan for being so honest with me because he could have taken the easy way out. I wanted to be successful at Warner Bros., and here was someone who was willing to help me by being honest with me. That was more than two decades ago, and to this day, I am very aware of coming into a place and the first impression I make on people. Instead of coming on overly strong, I try to ask questions of others and get to know them on a mutually respectful level.

What Is Self-Awareness?

Joel's story is a powerful example for several reasons:

- When he entered the meeting, he had good intentions.
- He presented himself as someone he wasn't (or at least an exaggerated version of himself).
- He had the courage to ask for feedback.
- His friend had the courage to be direct but kind.
- Rather than react defensively, he listened to the feedback and thanked Jordan for being honest.
- Maybe most importantly, he took the feedback to heart and looked for ways to implement it.
- These changes have helped Joel take his career and his relationships to a higher level.

Psychologists suggest that being self-aware involves having a conscious awareness of our traits (personality), behaviors, and feelings. I agree with that concept, but for me it is taking it one step further. It is being aware of the impact I have, especially my behaviors, on other people around me. As in Joel's story, sometimes we have the best intentions, but we can't know if we are being effective without being clued into the reactions of people and understanding their perspectives as well.

Be Yourself, But Pay Attention

To be clear, I am not suggesting you shouldn't be yourself. In fact, that's what got Joel into trouble in his story. I am suggesting that you should try to be your *best* you. Bring your gifts and skills to the table along with a new superpower—the ability to understand the impact you have on others.

It's about your mindset toward your own development. The first step is understanding what self-awareness is, and the second is believing that it can help rocket your potential.

Formal Methods for Increasing Self-Awareness

These days most organizations have a performance evaluation process, which usually focuses on whether you are meeting the business metrics for your role. If you're lucky, your company will equally value employee behaviors. Hopefully, you have an enlightened manager who will also see performance evaluations as an opportunity to offer behavioral feedback. If not, you should ask for it.

In my current role at Spectrum Reach, we realize that we have hundreds of team members at junior levels, and we want to make sure we provide some early personal and leadership development training for non-people managers. Many of the other organizations for which I have worked also offered a wide variety of opportunities like online or in-person courses to help people develop and increase their self-awareness. Ask your human resources department what is available and let them and your manager know you are interested in these opportunities.

Another great way to increase your self-awareness is by taking a 360-degree feedback assessment. This will allow your coworkers to provide feedback to you (most often anonymously) about your strengths as well as developmental opportunities. The advantage to these multi-rater assessments is that you can identify themes and patterns that you would like to address. You will invariably see a consensus about what people agree you do well. You will also see the flip side of any agreement about developmental needs. There is an old Yiddish proverb that says, "If one person tells you that you are a horse's backside, you can ignore them. If three people tell you that you are a horse's backside, go buy a saddle."

Finally, even if you are not able to participate in a course or receive 360-degree feedback, you should consider using a personality assessment to help you understand yourself better. Most human resources departments have people certified to use at least one kind of self-only assessment. Common ones include the MBTI, WorkPlace Big Five Profile, DiSC, Hogan, among others.

Informal Methods for Increasing Self-Awareness

I have coached young women who work for organizations—especially start-ups—where there is no formal performance appraisal process in place. The environment is more chaotic and in many cases, they are figuring everything out as they go. I encourage them to take the lead and initiate a conversation with their manager to ask for feedback about how they are performing their job and how they are working with others and within the culture of that organization. This is an opportunity to get beyond the "what I have done" to "how I am doing it."

Not all managers are alike. Some may be very forthcoming to offer personal feedback, and others might be more reluctant. Some might need a bit more structure, which you can provide by using specific, non-threatening question prompts. In the following examples the manager's name is Elizabeth, and she is only a couple of years older than the employee. She is a bit reserved and perhaps a little nervous about the session herself.

- "Elizabeth, as I go forward, can you suggest one thing that I could do differently to work better with you?" (This should make it easier for Elizabeth to comment because 1) she is only speaking for herself, not the entire work group, and 2) the employee has asked for one suggestion, so Elizabeth realizes that she can identify one thing— hopefully something high-impact.)

- "Have you noticed any of my behaviors or actions that you think are getting in my way of being as effective as I can be?"

- "What would you recommend I could do to improve my soft skills?"

  ....

- "What do you think is the most important thing I have to learn to do next to be effective?"

  ....

- "I would like to be seen as someone who gets and fits in with the company culture. What should I do more of or less of to improve my fit?"

This is not an exhaustive list, of course, but just a few examples to get the conversation started. Notice that these are not yes/no questions. Don't be afraid to ask for specifics if you are getting vague comments. Finally, once Elizabeth steps up with a nugget or two of feedback, the employee should let her off the hook, say thanks, and start thinking about how to implement any changes.

Another hugely valuable and available—but often overlooked—source for informal feedback is by asking a trusted colleague for feedback in the moment. That kind of conversation might look like this:

You: (while walking back to your office with a colleague immediately after a meeting with a prospective client) Tom, I don't think my part of that presentation went very well. What would you suggest I do differently next time?"

Tom: No, I thought you did okay. There was just kind of a weird low energy from everyone in the room." (Tom is your friend and isn't looking to make you feel worse about the meeting. You might have to push back a bit.)

You: Tom, come on, I need your help here. I have to do the same presentation next week in New York, and I trust your opinion on things like this.

Tom: Well, I guess I would definitely suggest one thing. I noticed that when the customers asked us questions, you interrupted them and started answering before they finished. I could tell they were getting frustrated. Let them finish, repeat their question back to them, *then* answer.

Just Ask Your Mother

Not all feedback has to be new and specific to your current job. What do you already know about yourself? How do your friends describe you when you aren't around? A friend of mine once told me that his mother gave him some feedback when he was a kid. Because his mother gave praise sparingly, it had a big impact when she did. She told him that she appreciated his ability to notice and describe something good he sees in everyone. My friend said that because of that feedback early on, he has tried to continue doing so all his life. (This also speaks to the power of timely feedback.)

Want to try it? I have included a simple worksheet that you can copy and distribute to ten people. Have them return them anonymously to one of your trusted colleagues. That colleague will then bring them to you for your review. No matter what, make sure to send out an email thanking everyone (even though you might not get 100% return and therefore might not know who returned worksheets on your behalf).

Sample feedback request email:

I am participating in an activity to increase my self-awareness and my effectiveness in the long-term. I am reaching out to a just a few people to get their responses. I have included you because I appreciate and value your opinion. When completed, please email to [name] by [date]. [Name] will compile these and return them to me. This is anonymous, and I will not know who said what. Thanks in advance for your help with this.

1. *If someone asked you, what is [your name] like to work with, how would you describe me in five words? Please include both upside and downside words that apply.*
2. *What are [your name]'s greatest strengths?*
3. *What are areas that [your name]'s could work to improve?*
4. *Is there anything else you would like to say that I have not asked about?*

Self-Awareness as a Superpower

There are lots of tips and suggestions in this book. In my opinion, none is more important than increasing your self-awareness. Why is it that so many people seem unaware of the impact their behaviors have on others? For one thing, it is not for the faint of heart.

To open yourself up to hear feedback from others requires a willingness to be vulnerable, and it runs counter to our normal routine of protecting ourselves from anything negative. But for those willing to take the risk, the reward is high. By making subtle tweaks to a selective behavior—while still being yourself—you can gain so much.

For most of us, hearing negative feedback is difficult. The thing is, even though it might be hard to hear in the moment, in the long run it can really be a gift. Don't believe me?

Try this:
Think about the last time someone gave you negative feedback—particularly if it caught you by surprise or was quite different from your own opinion.

1. *What was your internal reaction when they told you? What were you thinking?*
2. *It's now one day later. After reflecting on it for twenty-four hours, what are you thinking now?*
3. *It's now one week later. What are you thinking now?*

If you are like most people in this regard, you are at a very different place after you get some distance from the exchange and have time to reflect and consider the feedback more objectively. The point of this exercise is to know your own response cycle and understand that it is better to not respond in the moment.

Self-awareness involves not only a higher awareness of your strengths and weaknesses, but it also requires being an active observer of your own behavior in the moment. Think of it as a meta-behavior. For example, let's say that I have a hard time with people who ramble on and on and take forever to get to the point, if they ever do. When that happens, I get fidgety, cut people off, and sometimes say something like, "Can you just get to the point?" I know this gets in the way of my effectiveness and my relationships with coworkers, so I am working on being less rude to them. I must have a meta-level of observation when in the moment. I must be able to tell myself, "This is one of those times when you get impatient." In my mind, I send out a little drone that hovers above me and observes my interaction and sends me back signals about how I'm doing. After a while, it just becomes second nature.

You can see that increasing your self-awareness takes commitment, effort, and vulnerability. But it has a big payoff, and you can develop it into a superpower that will serve you in many aspects of your life, for the rest of your life.

Chapter Countdown
MAIN TAKEAWAYS FROM THIS CHAPTER:

- Understand what self-awareness is and why it's so important.
- Try both formal and informal ways to increase your self-awareness.
- Be open to honest feedback and willing to make changes in your behavior.
- If you make self-awareness a superpower, the results power your sustained success.
- Tweaking the way you behave and interact just a bit can make a huge difference.

CHAPTER 4

Find a Role Model, Be a Role Model

———————

What does the expression "role model" mean to you? *Merriam-Webster* defines a role model as ". . . a person whose behavior in a *particular role* is imitated by others."[1] The term was originally coined by sociologist Robert Merton in the 1950s, and it remains one of the cornerstones for our development as employees and as people. Merton made it clear that you didn't necessarily want to completely adopt the entire personality of your role models. He suggested, ". . . followers can pick and choose the characteristics they emulate, imitating the role model only in relation to a particular role and not worrying about other aspects of the role model's life."[2]

Role Models as a Tapestry of Influence

That's why I always considered my role models as a person—or tapestry of people—who inspires me to become my best personal and professional self. They do this by being the person they are. It is up to you to decide what behaviors or traits you admire and how you want to incorporate them into your own approach to work and life.

Besides role models, there are other kinds of helpful relationships that most of us create or encounter over our careers. It's probably a good idea to take a minute here to differentiate between them because they are often confused.

A *role model* is someone you look up to or admire for specific traits or skills. It could be anyone—someone you work with, a family member, or a famous leader you have never met. Often your role model has no idea you have decided they are your role model—unless you decide to tell them. You will probably have many role models over the course of your career because you can pick and choose what things you want to emulate from each. You might have one role model for public speaking, another for treating everyone with kindness, and another for strong organizational skills, and so on.

A *mentor*, by comparison, is more directly involved with you and interacts with you on a personal level. They take an active interest in your career and your goals and offer you help based on their own experience. A mentor offers advice, serves as a sounding board, and connects you with people who can help you or with whom you have common interests.

A *coach* is usually a professional hired by you or your organization to address a specific challenge or obstacle and to hold you accountable for making progress. The relationship is typically more transactional, focuses on development, and is contracted for a specific period.

A *sponsor* is someone who advocates for you behind closed doors. Typically, this would be someone who discusses your qualifications for a raise, special assignment, or promotion. In an article at *Forbes.com*, Ruth Gotian suggests that a mentor talks with you, a coach talks at you, and a sponsor talks about you.[3]

Where Does It Start?

Many of our first role models come from our inner circle of family and friends. My first role model—and the one that endures to this day—was my incredible mother, Laura. Beautiful, bright, and feisty, Mom was a force of nature. I was fortunate to have her as a guiding force and confidante for much of my adult life and I miss her every day. Now that I am the matriarch of our family, I often ask myself "What would Mom say or do?" before making a decision.

She had to help care for my grandparents and didn't have the opportunity to attend college, so she became a bookkeeper for a fashion company and did some modeling for them as well. After she married my dad, they worked together in the family business. And when they moved to Florida and Dad started a second career as a financial planner at Raymond James, they partnered on serving clients.

Mom was a fantastic example of a working mother. She and my dad were true partners as owners of the Rugby Sport Shop and worked hard and long hours. But she was always available and would come home on a moment's notice if we needed an extra dose of mothering.

Mom was a perfectionist and held herself and everyone to the highest standards. She was crazy clean, and insisted that my sister, Sharon, and I keep our shared bedroom in perfect shape. Although we complained as kids, of course, as adults, both of us are also crazy clean and neat. When my sister wants to good-naturedly tease me, she'll say, "You're acting just like Mom." I inherited Mom's perfectionism, and it took me many years to realize that being perfect is an unattainable and exhausting goal. Sometimes you may "try out" behaviors you admire in others but then evolve them into your own version of that trait. So, my goal is to always do my best and embrace not wanting to be perfect.

Another important role model for me from within my family was my dear Aunt Ruth. She sparked my love for reading and writing. When I was young, Aunt Ruth lived down the hallway in the same apartment building as us. She didn't have any children of her own and adored spending time with my sister and me.

To entertain us before we could read ourselves, she wrote enchanting stories and enthusiastically read them aloud. My favorite was about a dog named Taffy. She also took us to the neighborhood library after school, where we spent joyful hours exploring both classic and new children's books. For birthdays and special occasions, she lovingly crafted poems for family members. In honor of Aunt Ruth, I have carried on the poem-writing tradition for special family occasions. Take a moment to think back to people who uplifted you early on, as well as those close to you today.

Other great early role models can be our peers, teachers, professors, extended family, or even someone you follow on social media or the web. For me, it was my magazine-writing professor at Hofstra University who continually challenged me to stretch myself on assignments. Frank was a contributing writer for *New York* magazine, at the time known for its provocative articles, and later became an editor at *Black Enterprise* magazine. He motivated me to dig deeper to find and bring stories to life. In my years as a magazine editor, I modeled Frank's approach with my stable of freelance writers.

Professional Role Models

Once we enter the job world, bosses and work colleagues organically become role models. When you're in career-launch mode, it's especially important to model examples of professional behavior. In a tough job market, I landed my first job as an editorial assistant at *American Baby* magazine via an ad in the classified section of *The New York Times*. My dad suggested I send my cover letter and resume with a small photo of myself (looking professional with a big smile). Three weeks after my college graduation, our home phone rang. It was a personal phone call from the editor in chief of *American Baby*, asking me to come to New York City for an interview.

When I walked into the office at 575 Lexington Avenue, I was impressed and intimidated. Judith, who liked to be called Judy, was six feet tall and impeccably dressed. I came prepared to the interview with a portfolio of article clips from my college newspapers and *Bay News*, a local Brooklyn newspaper, that was my summer job during college. I listened intently, took notes, and sent an immediate thank-you note—another thing I learned from my role model mother. Less than a week later, Judy called and offered me my first full-time job. I was overwhelmed with joy—and fear. I will always be grateful to Judy for taking a chance on this Brooklyn girl.

Judy taught me essential skills for being a strong editor. Even more importantly, she was a role model for how a professional woman dressed and acted. I strived to emulate her style and grace. We had monthly editorial meetings at the charming French bistro Brasserie and celebrated the holidays at the elegant Russian Tea Room. She took me to meetings and luncheons at The American Society of Magazine Editors, where years later I was chosen to be a judge for their annual National Magazine Awards.

When Judy entered a room, whether it was for an internal, client, or industry meeting, everyone took notice. She smiled warmly and looked people straight in the eye, making them feel the center of her attention. She was poised and powerful. Later in my career, I learned this is called executive presence—and Judy was a model to me for honing and improving my own over my career.

The fact that my first boss was a wonderful role model was great fortune. But there are many ways to find role models of your own. The first step is to pay attention.

Become a Keen Observer

Who are people you admire the most? Who do you look up to? They may be family, friends, colleagues, athletes, celebrities, or humanitarians. And you don't need to only look for living role models. Some of the best may have been dead for centuries! Think about the reasons you admire them, and jot down a list of the qualities, personality traits, behaviors, or accomplishments that you strive to emulate. Ultimately, the person you want to admire is also yourself.

Be an active observer of others—the "role" of role models is to help you "see" examples of behaviors and successes that you want to adopt for yourself (or avoid). The people you work with, socialize with, or live with are offering you a living laboratory for you to observe at no risk to you. Pay attention, notice what works well and doesn't.

Look for role models who exemplify qualities and behaviors that align with your values. For me, the most positive role models are people who embody:

- Integrity
- Empathy
- Positivity
- Professionalism and strong work ethic
- Humility
- Optimism
- Strong communication skills
- An innate desire to be better
- Expertise in a particular subject
- A willingness to help others

Sometimes people you briefly encounter become lifelong inspirations.

Through a variety of professional and personal experiences, I am eternally grateful to have met and been energized by some amazing individuals:

- **Oprah Winfrey**—I met Oprah at a surprise fiftieth birthday party for our mutual friend, Joe, the director of The Oprah Winfrey Show. Oprah's energy and warmth were exhilarating. When my husband, Joel, asked if he could take a photo of us, she flung her arms around me with genuine glee. Being hugged by Oprah literally and figuratively reminds me that two self-made women are smiling in my cherished photograph. What I admire most about Oprah is that she came from humble means to become one of the most successful and philanthropic women in the world. To me, she is the ultimate self-made role model.

  ....

- **Hillary Clinton**—Joel and I met First Lady Hillary Clinton twice. The first time was at a children's health event at the White House. The second time was a couple of years after her unsuccessful bid for President at a New York City theater benefit. Although years and positions apart, she was equally engaging and engaged both times. What I most admire about Hillary is her resilience to weather and overcome countless political and personal challenges. You can be sure you will have bumps along your own way—that's part of personal and professional growth. Take each opportunity to analyze and learn from each of those situations. Ask yourself what you could have done differently or how you can meet the challenge put forth.

  ....

- **Christiane Amanpour**—At an intimate gathering of business leaders, award-winning journalist Christiane Amanpour spoke eloquently about her visit to the Middle East and her predictions about the possibilities for future peace in the troubled region. She also talked about life in New York City in between her global investigative reporting. When it came time for Q&A, I asked how she balanced reporting global news all over the world with normal family life. Her answer was simply, "At home, I still take out the garbage." Her answer was a wonderful example that our models can be both extraordinary and ordinary. You can achieve tremendous success and still remain grounded.

....

- **Francois Pienaar**—As Captain of the Springboks, the South African Rugby national rugby team, Francois helped unify South Africa to victory in the 1995 Rugby World Cup. This was the first major tournament to be held in post-apartheid South Africa. During this time of transformation, Francois developed a strong friendship with President Nelson Mandela, who became godfather to Francois's two sons. I had the good fortune to sit next to Francois at a members-only marketing organization dinner. He was charming and humble, but what most impressed me was how he moved beyond his apartheid upbringing to deliver a victory far beyond the game. Francois helped heal a nation through sport.

....

- **Madeleine Albright**—As a diplomat and the first female United States Secretary of State in US history (1997–2001 under President Bill Clinton), Madeleine Albright discovered the power of jewelry to convey a foreign policy message. For example, after Saddam Hussein's press referred to her as a serpent, Secretary Albright wore a golden snake brooch for her next meeting about Iraq. During her tenure, she collected more than 200 brooches, many of which are featured in her book *Read My Pins*, and have been exhibited all over the world.

When I met Secretary Albright at an executive business conference, she was wearing a bright blue suit and a beautiful bird pin. When I asked about her choice for the day, she said she was anticipating a free-flowing dialogue. From Secretary Albright I learned that you don't have to speak loudly—or sometimes at all—to be influential.

What all these role models have in common is tremendous fortitude and an unwavering desire to make the world a better place. Every day they inspire me to be a better person and to have a higher purpose. In many ways, that has been the driving force behind writing this book.

The other thing they have in common is that none of them is perfect. Each of them has detractors who are ready to point out perceived flaws in their behavior or character. That's the thing about identifying role models for yourself, you don't have to become the other person. As Robert Merton said, you get to select the qualities that you admire and want to emulate for yourself. That is why I like the idea of role models as a tapestry that takes shape or becomes a design as you weave in the best things about the people you meet on your life's journey.

The Anti-Role Model

Not all role models are positive. Have you seen someone at work implode due to bad behavior? What kind of coworker, boss, or other person do you *not* want to be? Sometimes negative role models can be helpful because they offer examples of harmful or disruptive behavior.

Research tells us that we can learn a lot from bad role models. A seminal study by the Center for Creative Leadership examined the ways in which people learn the most important lessons about leadership.[4] Not surprisingly, some of the most influential experiences we have are from exposure to other people. Role models—both good and bad—were reported to be highly influential. As you would expect, people reported learning a lot from positive role models. But fully one-third of the respondents reported learning important lessons from a rogue's gallery of bullying, tyrannical, and unpredictable bosses. The most frequent lesson reported was what *not* to do. The common consensus was, "If I ever get to that level, I will never treat people like that."

I have certainly seen that play out around me in many of the companies I worked for over the course of my career. I have witnessed countless examples of self-centered people who ultimately self-destructed. Not becoming like them became one of my strongest guiding principles. Even when I have been tempted to lose my cool, I remember those "must avoid" destructive behaviors, take a deep breath, and think carefully about my next step.

Aspire to Be a Role Model

Keep in mind that even as you seek to model the positive and avoid the negative behaviors you see in others, people will be looking to you to be a role model for them. As I mentioned earlier, this happens most often without you knowing it—often early in your career with your peers. As you gain experience and confidence, you increase the opportunities to be a positive influence on other people and your organization, friends, and family.

Sometimes everyday actions and approaches can motivate others. For example, at work, remember to say thank you to a team member who has done a great job on a challenging project. Smile and chat with your local neighborhood business owners and workers. Bring positivity and joy to your daily activities.

Chapter Countdown

MAIN TAKEAWAYS FROM THIS CHAPTER:

- Role models can be a tapestry of people.
- Write a list of people you most admire—and why.
- Be a keen observer of qualities you want to emulate.
- Anti-role models can teach you a lot about what not to do.
- Pay it forward by being a role model for others.

Section

2

BLAST OFF

CHAPTER 5
Excel by Being Passionately Curious

———

Do you want to stand out from the crowd, flourish, and build stronger professional and personal relationships? Then add *passionate curiosity* to your repertoire. As an aspiring magazine editor in college, the practice of asking good questions (known as the five Ws—who, what, where, why, and when) was drilled into me as the foundation of good journalism. Over the years I have found that this practice—combined with a strong desire to never stop learning—can be a real career booster. The following are some key tips to help you excel in both your business and personal life.

Prepare to Be Curious

With so much information at our fingertips, it's never been easier to be curious. Do your homework about the other person before any business interaction, whether it's via email, phone, video, or in person. LinkedIn makes it so easy to find out if you already have connections or things in common. Perhaps you went to the same school, have the same hobbies, have kids the same age, know people in common, or have interests that match—all potential conversation starters. Check whether someone is a thought leader who writes blog posts or is quoted as a business expert. It's always impressive when someone takes the time to find out something important to me, like my passion for coaching and mentoring. This sounds so basic, but it is shocking how often people don't put in the extra effort. You can differentiate yourself by being passionately prepared.

Be Genuinely Interested in Other People

Questions are the heart and soul of communication and learning. Answers are the big payoff. There are two different types of questions, based on whether you are trying to get to know someone better on a business or personal level. It's usually a good idea to start with business or career-focused questions. Here are some icebreakers:

- How did you get to where you are now?
- What qualities have made you successful?
- Did you set out to work in this kind of business?
- What challenges have you had to overcome in your career?
- What are some of the other companies you have worked for?
- How has your company or function (e.g., marketing, sales, or communications) changed over the last year . . . or last five years?
- What trends do you see in this business or industry?
- What do you love about your job . . . this business?
- What are some of your biggest challenges these days?
- What keeps you up at night?
- How can I be of most help to you?

If you establish a strong rapport with someone on a business level, you may be intrigued to get to know them better on a personal level as well. Some engaging and thought-provoking questions to ask may be:

- Where did you grow up?
- What was your first paying job?
- How would your best friend describe you?

- When are you the happiest?
- What inspires you?
- If I paid for you to get a new degree, what subject would it be in?
- What don't you know how to do that you would like to learn?
- If money was no object but you still had to work, what would you do for a living?
- What is your favorite book, movie, TV show, artist, celebrity, or vacation spot?

Lean in and listen enthusiastically to the answers. Many people are flattered and enjoy talking about themselves, whether on a business or personal level. Sometimes you may encounter someone who is reluctant to open up on any level. If, and when, that's the case, read the tea leaves and try to figure out how to get into their comfort zone. If you are truly interested and remember details about a person, you might come across an article or other information that addresses something the two of you discussed or that you think they would appreciate knowing about. It's a great way to stay in touch in a genuine way and show that you remember them.

Be Curious About Your Organization

Passionate curiosity isn't just about people, it can be about anything. Be an expert on your own organization. Again, find out details by doing some of research. How did it start? Many well-known companies have surprising origins. For example, McDonald's started as a hot dog stand at an airport. IBM was the result of a merger of three companies that produced meat slicers, scales, and computer punch cards. Toyota originally built and sold weaving looms. In addition to its roots, here are some things you should probably know about your organization:

- What are your leading products/services?
- What are the high-level financials?

- Who are your three main competitors? How is your company different?
- What is your organization's mission?

Be a Student of the World

Have some entertaining nuggets to talk about at a cocktail party, in the back of an Uber, or even in a virtual happy hour. Spend time gathering information about a wide variety of subjects. Everyone likes interesting and likeable people. Know a little bit about what's going on in media, world affairs, science, politics, sports, pop culture, and even the latest Kardashian caper. Blogs and websites can be inspiring sources of information. Some of my favorites are:

- **theSkimm.com**—A morning newsletter that connects the dots on the day's biggest stories

....

- **TrendHunter.com**—Spark new ideas with the world's #1 largest trend platform

....

- **theHUSTLE.com**—Business and technology in five minutes or less

....

- **BusinessInsider.com**—Business site with deep information on financial, media, technology, and other industry verticals

Sometimes these common interests are substantial, like politics or a common cause. We tend to overlook small connections that can have impact. You can use these nuggets as icebreakers. I once made a memorable first impression with someone who became a client. When I discovered he was a baseball fan, I asked, "What duo has their work featured but are not inducted as members in the Baseball Hall of Fame?" Even most baseball fans don't know the answer (see answer at the end of this chapter). We connected about something that piqued his interest, and the connection continues to this day. Another fun sports question is: what are the only two days of the year in which there are no professional sports games? The answer is the day before and after Major League Baseball's All-Star Game every year in July.

Even a brief connection can entice people to gravitate toward us more than we realize. Research shows that we are much more likely to form connections with whom we have even small things in common. For example, one study showed that people who simply share the same initials are 11% more likely to connect than those who do not.[5] Once you start looking for what you have in common with others (instead of how you are different) it can become second nature.

Be Selfish

Finally, have fun being passionately curious—doing it for yourself. For example, I walk around with my iPhone and use voice memo to note everything I don't understand or want to know more about in a day. This could be the definition of a word, a new app that proclaims to change the way we think, or the Buddhist monk philosophy. For example, while trying to add more substance and "flesh out" this chapter, I wondered where the term came from and learned that "flesh out" is believed to come from the idea of adding flesh, or physical substance, to a skeleton or a frame. Eww. I never realized that when my college journalism professor asked me to flesh out an article!

Some people are naturally curious, but you can build the discipline into your daily routine. Whenever you have a few minutes, continuously fertilize your knowledge base. Do this to feed your own curiosity, starting with your newly found knowledge that Abbott and Costello were recognized by the Baseball Hall of Fame for their iconic "Who's on First?" comedy routine.

Chapter Countdown
MAIN TAKEAWAYS FROM THIS CHAPTER:

- Dig deep. Don't be satisfied with surface knowledge of your company, its products and services, customers, and your fellow employees.
- Take the lead on connecting with people. Keep a repertoire of genuine questions handy.
- Stay current on local, national, and world events—especially those that will impact your organization and coworkers.
- Listen to people and find common ground—it's a great place to build from.
- Be selfish, and enjoy the process of expanding your knowledge and awareness.

CHAPTER 6
Work Smarter and Harder Than Anyone Else

How many times have we heard, "Work smarter, not harder"? It's one of those catchphrases people love to say, as if that explains everything. The problem is, they seldom tell us how. If they do make suggestions, they tend to be specific examples of the things that worked for them. Fair enough, right? Most people mean well, especially if they see that you are struggling. The challenge is that working smarter is not a one-size-fits-all proposition. Like so many things we talk about in this book, working smarter begins with an open and honest look at yourself. If you are struggling with your workload or your energy at work, ask yourself why. Once again, self-awareness is the superpower that seems to touch almost every chapter in this book.

Easy to Say, Harder to Understand

Plenty of people work hard. If you do, people might notice you are a hard worker. Or, if you're the kind of person who works your tail off quietly behind the scenes, you could be overlooked. A former mentee and now close family friend of mine named Candace, a successful manager of digital marketing at Campbell's, told me, "Sometimes for a woman it's not enough just to work hard." (By the way, more on Candace in the next chapter). What she meant was that you must be savvy and strategic to make the hard work count. The people who stand out are those willing to go the extra mile and roll up their sleeves and get the job done. But it is also being savvy enough to know that not everything on your plate is of equal importance. Going the extra mile to make a customer happy carries more weight than going the extra mile to make sure the PowerPoint you are working on is formatted so that the right margin is 1/32 of an inch rather than 1/16. Maybe I'm exaggerating for effect, but some of you reading this are smiling because I am describing you.

My experience has been that you must work smarter *and* harder.

As I mentioned, there are a lot of hard workers in organizations, and advancement requires it. But there is a tipping point in one's career where people begin to recognize you as someone who thinks for yourself and has good ideas. That tipping point is about moving from the physical work to creative thinking, and I believe it is happening earlier in one's career nowadays than ever before. To get there, you must work smarter. But what does that mean?

What Is It That Smart People Do Differently?

Smart people are self-aware. They are not afraid to take an open and honest look at their strengths and weaknesses, which I prefer to call areas for development and/or improvement. Smart people are not afraid to ask for feedback. If they are not sure about what they do well or not so well, they ask others. This might come in the form of informal, in-the-moment feedback, or more formal feedback like a 360-degree assessment. Smart people leverage their strengths. They use the things they do well to strengthen relationships and to provide the maximum contribution they can make to their work group. Smart people address their development or improvement areas. But they don't try to tackle all of them all at once. They pick the most important one and then craft a plan. That may come through mentoring, formal training, reading, and trying things out, or other activities. Once they feel they have successfully addressed that needed improvement, they decide if they want to tackle another one. Smart people understand that they might not be able to change everything about themselves. As hard as it is for us to admit, sometimes it is a better idea to delegate to a coworker with better skills in that area. For example, while I'm a strong presenter, I rely on others to design the accompanying PowerPoint presentations if needed. If you are especially strong in certain areas like PowerPoint, Photoshop, or Excel, for example, volunteer to help those who aren't as proficient. It can be a great value exchange with a more senior colleague or even your boss!

Understand Your Own Work Style

Sometimes working smarter it isn't about strengths and weaknesses. Sometimes it is about your personal work style. In that case, a task left uncompleted might not be about a lack of skill, but about *how* you are approaching it. If you think about the ways you could work smarter, it might be because of the work or tasks you are avoiding because they are difficult for you, or you just don't like doing them. Understand your own work style and the way it dovetails with your job responsibilities. Here are some of the ways I have seen successful colleagues work smarter:

- Be realistic about how long things take. Anticipate and block your schedule appropriately.

- Face the reality of your work window. How much time do you, personally, have available to tackle the task? Is it enough? Do you need to engage someone else's help?

- Farm out other tasks to make way for this one. Use this as an opportunity to delegate work you might otherwise cling to.

- Focus the time you have available on the things that will make the most difference.

  ....

- Know your own energy cycles. What time are you highest energy? When does your energy lag? When are you most creative?

  ....

- If you know you are running out of gas by the end of the day, save that time for tasks that don't require deep thinking.

  ....

- Eliminate distractions. Close your door (if you have one). Turn off the chime that signals incoming email. Forward your phone.

  ....

- Know the difference between urgent and important and try to stay focused on the important.

  ....

- Request clarity of instructions when taking on a task. So much time can be wasted going back for clarity or even going down the wrong path before you actually are working on the right thing.

(Don't) Rage Against the Machine

Every organization has electronic systems for getting work done. Some of them, like Microsoft Teams, Zoom, or SAP, are commercial products— possibly modified to work in your organization. Others are internal systems designed by your IT team or a contractor and customized specifically for your organization's use. These systems are easy to learn and make both the quality and efficiency of your work better. At least, that's the theory. The reality is that many times these systems are overly complicated, balky, and bloated with features you will never use. Guess what, you must learn them anyway. Invest your time and energy into learning what you need to get your work done. Set aside time. Ask for help. Befriend your key IT colleagues, some of the most valuable and often underappreciated members of the team. A holiday gift and a special thank you can go a long way—and help expedite attention to your needs and challenges. Write your own version of instructions down. It sure beats the alternative, which is complaining about it instead of learning it. Get onboard, and just do it. Besides, in a year there will probably be a new system to replace that one.

Did You Get That Email I Sent You?

A McKinsey report showed that we spend 28% of our time at work reading, writing, and responding to email.[6] That's thirteen hours in a typical week. Because email has so thoroughly taken over some of our lives, it gets its own section in this chapter about working smarter. Think about that for a minute. If you are like most people, most emails you receive are about other people's agendas. If you are spending that much time working on other people's agendas, when do you work on your own agenda? Test my theory. Look at your last twenty emails. Whose agenda are they moving forward?

When you write an email, it's important to choose your words carefully and intentionally. And before you hit that send button, it's a good idea to proofread that email through the eyes of the receiver. One of my former bosses gave me an extremely constructive piece of advice about the unintentional impact an email can have. He called me into his office, where, on his desk, he had a printed copy of an update I had sent him about a current project. He handed me the email and asked, "What do you think is wrong with this email?" While rereading it, I noticed that several sentences began with the word "I," He said, "That's right, you should replace every reference to "I" with "we." Of course, it was not my intent to take all the credit, and it was embarrassing to read the email from everyone else's perspective. Eternally grateful for the sage advice, I have given it to many of my own direct reports and mentees. To this day, I am a stickler when people send out emails (or even in conversations) that overuse "I" instead of "we."

While emails are the reality of our world and we all probably feel like we get too many, there are ways to exert some control.

- Turn off alerts that notify you of a new email received. That will reduce the odds that you will be distracted. Going back to what you were working on takes time to refocus and increases the chances of forgetting something or making a mistake.

....

- Don't default to email, unless it is a super short email response to someone. Pick up the phone and call. If you are in the office, go talk to the person. Doing those two things can accelerate closure on issues and reduce the back-and-forth by email.

....

- Maybe your emojis aren't enough. Remember that emails can increase the chance of being misunderstood.

....

- Be savvy about when to not use email. Never use email to cover your backside. Don't hide behind email to deliver bad news. Don't CC someone's boss just to get that person to take action.

....

- Block out a specific time each day to read and respond to email. Stick with it. For example, I scan my email first thing in the morning to identify priority and timely matters, which require immediate attention. And at the end of the workday, I catch up on less important emails and clean out my email box to keep it manageable.

....

- Unsubscribe to email blogposts, e-newsletters, promotional material, or anything else that you never open. You may want to have a separate email address for these types of communications so they don't clog your main email box and you can access them as needed.

Don't Reinvent the Wheel

People who work smart have no problem using or continuing work that has already been completed by others. To not start everything from scratch, they ask themselves and others, "What work has already been done on this? Is there a formatted PowerPoint template already created? Did we create a similar report last year for our financials? Have we done other work for previous clients that could serve as a starting point?"

Ask for Help

Working smarter involves not always going it alone. An important mindset change for a lot of people is to begin to see other people's time as a resource that you can and should tap into. People often confuse going it alone as the rugged individualist. That person is going to be working harder, but unnecessarily so. What can you delegate, buy, or drop?

Joel's Take

The most important aspect of working smarter is knowing how to ask for help and whom to ask. For me, it was not merely asking for help with my workload. That was in MY hands. I always wanted to understand what was behind the scenes of the brands and companies I worked for. For example, when I was in sales roles, it was vital to my success and self-esteem to truly understand the brands, products, or services I was pitching. Not so much about the specifications, but more about the story behind the product and the role of every professional colleague who brought that product/service to market. What was their relationship to the product? What were their pain points, and how could I help them? I had to go around and ask. Nobody just walked up to me and offered. I was always successful in meeting or exceeding sales goals. But it wasn't enough for me. I wanted to be part of a team and not just work in isolation. I discovered that other people's time and expertise were resources that I coveted to enhance my job skills and contributions. The only way I could do that was by asking others to help make me smart. For example, when I went to work at Marvel Comics as the senior vice president of corporate sales, I was in charge of selling the licensing and promotional rights for all the Marvel characters. I was surprised when a meeting with the creative team wasn't on the schedule as part of my orientation. My mission was to convince companies to buy the rights to use these characters in everything from commercial tie-ins to cereal to fast-food restaurants. Sure, I knew the basic back story. Every kid knew Spider-Man was really Peter Parker and that he got his Spidey powers when he was bitten by a radioactive spider. I wanted to know more and at a deeper level. I approached the artists who drew Spider-Man and the other characters and asked for their help. I met with the writers behind the characters to learn their stories. I learned from them about Marvel head writer Stan Lee's motivation for creating Spider-Man and what kind of impact he wanted Spider-Man to have on the reader. I didn't wait for that knowledge and relationships to come to me—I went after it myself.

That made me much more effective at talking with a potential customer or collaborator about our products. They knew me as someone with deep knowledge who wasn't just bullshitting about the characters from reading a couple of paragraphs. I knew exactly why Spider-Man was created, who Spider-Man was, and why Spider-Man connected with young people. It also gave me immediate credibility with the people behind the superhero storylines at Marvel. They knew that I respected their vision and that I had their backs. Sure, I wanted to exploit these icons but not at the expense of their inner essence. It was about working harder because I had to make the effort to establish relationships and ask others for their help. But by doing so, everyone benefitted in the end. And I acted as a true pro.

Letting Go

Working smarter means knowing when it is time to let something go completely. Is it time to kill a project that has proven to be a bust? Maybe it was someone else's pet project and everyone assumed it untouchable. Maybe it was a good idea back when the project started, but technology or demand has shifted away. Know when it is time to pull the plug on work that is no longer viable

For younger employees who may not have control over organizational projects, think about it on a personal workload level. What tasks are you doing that you could stop? I worked with a colleague early in my career who I will call Nancy. No one on our team was a smarter or harder worker, and one day she did something that made a huge impression on me. We were in a meeting with our boss, and he turned to Nancy and told her he was putting her in charge of creating a series of blog posts for a new customer. She diplomatically replied, "Mike, there are seven things I am working on right now that take up all of my time." She then quickly named each project. She continued, "I would be happy to write those posts, but what do you suggest we take off my plate to make room?" We were all kind of stunned and waited for the Mike's reaction. He chuckled and said, "Easy. Let's stop doing the staff newsletter you were doing. These blog posts for the client are much more important. Besides, I don't think anyone reads that newsletter anymore." I have used that strategy many times over the years. It also made me aware of proactively taking things off the plates of people who work for me whenever needed. That positions people to be able to work smarter *and* harder themselves.

Chapter Countdown

MAIN TAKEAWAYS FROM THIS CHAPTER:

- Hard work is the cost of admission, but it takes more than that to stand out.
- Understand your own work style and the ways you work best and most productively. People vary widely in this regard.
- Become good at using your organization's internal systems. Don't fight them and complain about them.
- Don't confuse busy with working smart. Watch out for the email trap.
- Know when it is time to let a project go completely to make room for more important work.

CHAPTER 7
Pay Your Dues

─────

It's too bad that the work world isn't like youth soccer. If it was, as soon as you graduate from college, you would get a trophy—plus your dream job. The reality is that you have to start a lot closer to the bottom and work your way up. That might happen slowly, quickly, or maybe not at all. There are no guarantees. The good news is that if you are willing to pay your dues, it greatly increases your chances of eventually ending up where you want to be—and maybe more.

Sometimes You Need to Take Two Buses

My first paying summer job (hourly minimum wage) taught me a valuable lesson. I had to take the bus and had to hassle with transferring from one route to another to get to work. The store was a women's clothing chain in Brooklyn called Joyce Leslie. My responsibilities included working in the dressing room, putting racks of clothes back on the floor, and sweeping up at the end of the night.

The extra spending money was nice, especially as a teenager, but I disliked the job and found it boring. When I complained to my parents, they challenged me to find the positive. So, I motivated myself to remember where every item of clothing went on the store floor and became the most efficient employee at putting clothes back. To this day, I'm an expert at hanging clothes up in record time. My closets were well organized way before Marie Kondo.

What does "taking two buses" really mean? It means that whatever job you do, even a menial job, do it exceptionally well. It means you sometimes need to do something you don't necessarily like, whether it's enduring two buses to get to work or engaging in mundane tasks. You never know what can happen or how your life can be influenced by just having the right attitude.

At a recent "speed mentoring" event for college students and recent graduates who aspire to be in the media and entertainment industry, one of the mentors summed things up well when she advised, "Do the small things well before you get picked for the big things."

Someone Might Notice

Remember Candace, the woman I mentioned in the last chapter? When we were touring college campuses for our son, Andrew, we met Candace. She was an enthusiastic sophomore who was earning spending money as a tour guide for prospective students. We were immediately impressed by her knowledge, passion, and genuine warmth. After the tour, we continued our lively conversation and learned she was a marketing major. Her personality exuded energy and positivity that made a big impression on us.

Candace acted as a "big sister" to Andrew during his freshman year. I was so impressed with her that I hired her as a summer intern and then for her first job after college. Today, many years later, Candace is a rising star at Campbell's and the mom of three beautiful young children. We recently referred a college student to her for industry and career advice. The lesson to learn from Candace is that whatever you do, give it your all! You never know when someone might notice and positively impact your life and career path.

Know Your Own Work Ethic

Sometimes hard work supersedes everything else. A strong work ethic is one thing that can make you valuable and invaluable. People will invest more time, energy, and money in team members who get things done, no matter how big or small. Those are certainly the team members I go the extra mile for. As you grow your career, never lose sight of how a small gesture can make a large impact. Be the person who says, "Happy to help in any way," and mean it. Volunteer for unglamorous assignments no one else might want. Step up and get it done while everyone else is just talking or complaining.

Seek Help from Others

Challenge yourself to become more proficient at tasks you may not necessarily enjoy. Seek help from others. For example, as an idea person, working with numbers and spreadsheets has always been tedious for me. However, it is a critical part of being able to bring ideas to life. Over the years, savvy finance colleagues have been great tutors and partners for me. It's amazing how learning to do something well can make that task more pleasant. And remember, somewhere on your career journey, you may need to take two buses. Jump on!

Chapter Countdown
MAIN TAKEAWAYS FROM THIS CHAPTER:

- You have to start somewhere, and sometimes you have to do things you don't like.
- Be the best you can be at whatever you do.
- Look, act, and be respectful.
- Accept that in every job, there will be aspects of it that you don't like to do. Challenge yourself to find the positive.
- Do the best job you can, not matter how menial. Be humble, and pay your dues.

CHAPTER 8
Bring a Unique Spark

———

Think beyond the skills that you bring to your job. What is it about you as a person that you bring to the mix? It's what I call your unique spark, and it is partly made up from your personality, somewhat from your self-awareness, your willingness to take risks, and your creativity.

Joel's Take

At one point in my career, I was head of marketing for celebrity chef David Burke's organization. David owned eight restaurants and was a regular guest on all the major Food Network TV shows. He was—and still is—one of the top chefs in the United States and is recognized as incredibly creative and innovative. He's known as "The Culinary Prankster."

We were hiring a part-time assistant and interviewed many people for the job. We gave each of them some kind of task as part of the selection process. One young woman we interviewed was named Julia. It just so happened that we were incredibly busy getting ready for a high-profile fundraising event for a not-for-profit organization where twenty of the top chefs in the world would have a booth and showcase their signature dishes. Everyone would be there, including Emeril, Bobby Flay, Daniel Boulud, and many other world-renowned chefs. Donors would pay an entrance fee to meet these famous chefs, sample their culinary creations, and the proceeds would go to charity. David didn't want to just cook at his booth. He decided to bring a Wizard of Oz theme to life with delicious offerings that he affectionately named scarecrow snails, cowardly lion burgers, and yellow brick road cake. The event was quickly approaching, and we needed someone to help greet people at the booth, introduce the dishes, and keep things moving.

We asked Julia what she was doing that day, and she said it didn't matter—she would be there to help. We said great, gave her the logistics of time and place, and challenged her to think of a way to help our booth stand out. She asked, "Well, what if I dress like Dorothy?" We ran it past David, and he thought it sounded good. I told her I was so busy getting ready for the event and that she would have to deal with finding an outfit herself.

Lo and behold, we're setting up the booth, and in walks Julia—dressed exactly like Dorothy, complete with pigtails, a blue plaid dress, and even a basket with a stuffed Toto dog in it. She even had ruby red slippers to complete the look. David went nuts and told me to hire her right away, which we did soon after.

To me this is a great example of someone going above and beyond, taking a risk, and adding a spark that not everyone could ignite with or pull off. When I left David's company and moved on to my next job, Julia eventually moved up to marketing manager and continued to bring her unique spark to every event afterward. Julia's career has continued to thrive, and as her LinkedIn profile proclaims, she is currently "a driven, organized, passionate foodie working in tech."

Attitude Can Be More Important Than Skills

Joel's story is a great example of bringing a unique spark. What was it that Julia did to add substance and value for Joel and David?

- She committed to the project.
- She was willing to take a risk.
- She identified a creative way to bring an idea to life (Dorothy!).
- She tested her idea quickly with Joel.
- She took responsibility for her costume and didn't add to Joel's workload.
- She executed the idea flawlessly.
- She exceeded everyone's expectations.

Positively Positive

We can't all channel Dorothy, but there are many ways you can stand out. One of the best ways to bring a spark is to be a positive person. This may sound obvious, but it's surprising how many times people choose to be negative. If you focus your cognitive energy on the negative, it reduces your ability to take the long view and generate alternative possibilities. Strive to embrace positivity and avoid negativity.

Personality in Play

Perhaps most importantly, a dour, pessimistic, and gloomy attitude will drive people away. Not even Winnie the Pooh could stand to spend all day with Eeyore, and coworkers don't want to work with someone who brings them down. Soon that person finds themself more and more on the outside of the group just because they are a downer.

One of my very first bosses used to have what she described as a "wince test." She said, "If you see someone standing outside your door and you wince, it's not a good sign. If you wince, it's usually because you know if that person is bringing you a problem and complaint, not a solution or idea." Way back then—and to this day—my commitment was to be an employee who makes my boss smile, not wince. My goal is for my bosses, colleagues, and direct reports to always be happy to see or talk to me because of my positive spark.

My dad used to talk about the impact of negativity on him. He said if he was walking down the street and saw, off in the distance, someone he knew coming toward him, he would make a decision. If it was someone who always had a cloud over their head and he knew would take up his time complaining about everything, he would cross over to the other side of the street to avoid the negative vibe.

When something bad happens, ask yourself, "What is one good thing that will come out of this?" It can reframe the way you handle setbacks, and it can help you see past the event or incident. I know this might be easier for some than others. Personality psychologists agree that certain personality traits, like optimism, are shaped roughly equally by genetics and by our early life experiences—usually before age seven. It stands to reason that if you inherit pessimistic genes and are brought up in a negative-focused environment, it might be more of a challenge for you to maintain optimism than someone else. But it can be done.

I'm not talking about adopting a naïve, overly rosy outlook. Having a positive mental attitude, a concept popularized by author Napoleon Hill, is the philosophy that having an optimistic perspective in every situation in one's life creates positive changes and increases effectiveness and accomplishments. Let's face it, it's not all sweetness and light at work, but there are tactics you can use to maintain a positive attitude. Always strive to see the glass as half full. As needed, change your framing to see things with a glass-half-full attitude as opposed to seeing the glass as half empty. Technically the glass is BOTH half empty and half full, but it's how you look at it that often determines the outcome.

- Focus on the good things. Don't overlook small positive things that are happening around you. You're not ignoring the challenging or difficult issues. You are just putting the positive on your radar. Notice them. Mention them to others.

- Practice gratitude. Start each day on a positive note by keeping a gratitude journal. Research has shown that expressing gratitude:[7]

  1. Improves happiness
  2. Reduces stress
  3. Has a positive impact on your health
  4. Strengthens personal relationships[8]

- Spend time with positive people. That attitude can rub off. Spending too much time around people with negative attitudes can be contagious.

- Practice positive self-talk.

- Identify your areas of negativity. We all have triggers. Knowing yours can help you keep from going into a spiral when they occur.

Assume Positive Intent

My friend Craig had a colleague once who would tell stories that all seemed to end with the phrase ". . . and that's how they get you." She had conditioned herself to mistrust everybody, and it seemed like she was playing defense against the entire world. Granted, nobody was ever going to pull a fast one on her, but it seemed to me like that would be a heavy burden to carry around. If you're going to assume anything, assume that, in general, most people act with positive intent (at least what they believe is the right thing to do). When someone says something or does something that affects us, it is so easy for us to make up a story in our own heads. In this story the other person is usually the bad guy, and we are the victims of their actions. Try assuming the other person meant well. It sounds like a small thing, but it can really change your mental framework.

Share a Passion

Bringing a unique spark often involves giving people the opportunity to see into your unique personality. What are you passionate about? I feel like I must make a caveat here about passion. It might be something that doesn't have anything to do with work but gives others an insight about what makes you tick. A current colleague of mine named Ben is an avid reader. He regularly takes the time to create and post an extensive list of his latest recommendations to share with family, friends, and colleagues. As the executive sponsor of my company's mentoring program, I was impressed with Ben's passion for learning and invited him to become a key member of our Mentoring Program Committee. His passion is infectious, and he adds tremendous value to our evolving program.

Any organization is a system with interdependent parts. Sales helps production, marketing helps recruiting, manufacturing helps sales, and so on. Think outside your narrow functional group. How can you help people in another group or department? Sometimes it seems like a small gesture, but it adds a spark. Send an article that will be helpful to others. Cheer each other on. Plan your week in a way that will be helpful to others. After a time, people will notice that spark.

Raise Your Hand

It's another form of positivity. Be willing to do more than your share and be willing to roll up your sleeves and take on the non-glamorous assignments.

For example, conduct loads of background research and create a spreadsheet with every detail to jumpstart a new project. Or proactively take thorough notes at a group meeting and circulate them immediately afterwards to the entire team.

In summary, attitude can be just as important as skillset. Are you a naturally positive person? Recognize that natural asset in yourself and look for ways to deploy it. Do you suspect you might be a more pessimistic person? You can't change your personality, but you can change your behavior by reframing how you look at things. It requires self-awareness and emotional intelligence (monitoring yourself in the moment), but the reward is great.

Chapter Countdown
MAIN TAKEAWAYS FROM THIS CHAPTER:

- You have attributes and attitudes that make you unique. What are they?
- Being positive while being realistic can energize others.
- Assume others mean well. It completely changes your approach.
- Share yourself and your interests and passions.
- Don't be afraid to jump in—even if something isn't directly a part of your job.

CHAPTER 9
Value Customer Service

There is a lot of commotion in the news nowadays about how colleges and universities are not teaching the practical skills that people will need early in their careers. This is particularly true for students in more traditional schools or majoring in non-business areas. When LinkedIn analyzed the postings for open positions, there were certain skills in demand across all industries in early-career jobs. These skills were not specifically taught in college but can help people stand out from the crowd and create a strong foundation for future roles. It was no surprise to me that customer service was at the top of the list.

According to Emily Poague, vice president of marketing at LinkedIn, "Employees who know how to ensure that customers feel valued, especially as many services are conducted online without that face-to-face element, are in high demand. In fact, we found the role of customer service specialist to be one of our top entry-level jobs right now."[9]

Businesses exist because of their customers, and customer service is all about being a true partner with your customers. A lot of organizations claim to treat the customers as a high priority, but the customer might experience something quite different. How many times have we been put on indefinite hold only to hear the disembodied voice continue to repeat, "Your call is very important to us . . ."? It sure doesn't make me feel important. In fact, it's quite the opposite.

The Partnership of Customer Service

In my current business, we're all about building what we call multi-screen advertising solutions for clients. The name of my group is the Client Success team. Our mission is to make sure that our internal customers—the sales organization and all our sellers and account executives—put together the right solutions for our clients. That means it's all about what our clients' goals and objectives are. We work hard to understand what they really need from the tools in our tool kit. Do they need TV advertising, streaming video, advanced advertising products online, or something else? And, although we have sales goals for each of these different products, the way we deliver the best customer service and the best solution for our clients is to understand from their perspective what they need. Then our job is to put together a solution that's right for them and execute that solution flawlessly.

The Customer Is Always Right (Until They Aren't)

For example, we might have a small business owner who wants to see their TV commercial on Monday Night Football. That sounds great but it might not be the best bang for their buck, and we may be able to find that the same target audience for them on other programs at more effective costs. It's all about understanding your customers' goals and objectives and how you genuinely and selflessly put together the solutions or the decisions that are truly right for them.

I have always urged my team to be totally honest and up front with customers. Even if you don't close a sale, you're still gaining an advocate who can recommend you to somebody else because of your sheer honesty. As a manager I'm willing to keep trying to find the right solutions for my clients because client satisfaction inevitably leads to sales success.

Service is the new economy, and people now expect tremendous service as well as honesty and transparency. Clients as consumers have more information at their fingertips than ever before. They will often know just as much as you do about the product or service you provide. We are all now influenced by "the Amazon effect." Free shipping, next-day delivery, and unquestioned returns are now the expectation. Superior customer service is now an expectation, and organizations will continue to hire and promote people who get it—and deliver it.

A big part of customer service is establishing yourself as a trusted advisor. The role is foremost a consultative partner, but it's also having the passion and commitment to really "wow" and delight the customer.

We're All in the Customer Service Business

If you're a young person in your first or second job, regardless of what your title is, there's likely some aspect of sales in your job. Even if you aren't dealing with external customers, at some point you're going to have to sell an idea or communicate effectively with your superiors. The brand that you establish internally in your early jobs is based on the degree to which you deliver on your commitments. You want to be someone people can count on, and that process starts internally with the people you work with. It is a terrific way to stand out from the rest of the pack. Be super reliable and trustworthy. Always deliver—and ideally over deliver.

You also must be a bit of a psychologist to understand whom you're dealing with and how they're feeling and thinking. You must be comfortable asking questions to learn where they're coming from and what's important to them. At the end of the process, what's important to almost everyone is that you're honest, open, and willing to listen.

The Power of Feeling Listened To

A study from the Federal Reserve Bank of New York found that only 27% of college graduates work in a field related to their major.[10] As a result, many people find themselves in direct customer service roles early in their careers with limited training or experience. There is an array of customer service training opportunities available within many companies as well as available free online. These are great ways to learn some of the basics, as well as useful tips and suggestions, to ramp up your customer service skills.

One of the most powerful skills you can have is making a customer feel listened to. We often leap into problem-solving mode too early, and the customer feels frustrated because you didn't listen completely to their problem. One of the most important things you can do is pause and reflect what you hear the customer saying back to them, then repeat what you heard for confirmation and validation. For example, "If I understand you, you are saying . . ." or "Let me understand what it is that you're asking for." These are good techniques for the customer to be confident that they were heard. It is also possible that they didn't phrase their question or concern clearly, and when they hear you repeat it back, it gives them an opportunity to rephrase it more accurately.

The next step is to explain what you are going to do about their problem. Be clear about what you will do. For example, "I will do everything I can to see if that's possible. However, it might not be possible. If that is the case, I will find another alternative that you feel is acceptable." Another effective approach to solving a customer's issues is to offer alternatives. Explain options a, b, and c, and let the customer select. Choice gives the customer a sense of control. Most importantly, do what you said you would do, and then follow up immediately.

The bottom line is that you want to be someone who builds trust with the customer. And the best way to do that is to listen and do what you say you are going to do.

Chapter Countdown

MAIN TAKEAWAYS FROM THIS CHAPTER:

- Understand what it truly means to be a partner with your customers.
- Your customers need you to be a trusted advisor. Collaborate with them as thinking partners.
- No matter what your title is, you are in the customer service business.
- Know how to listen to your customers.
- Many companies pay lip service to customer satisfaction. Go deeper and delight your customers by exceeding their expectations.

CHAPTER 10
Ask for Expert Advice

Having a career is not a solo act. In previous chapters we addressed the importance of other people, including how to build your network and find a mentor. This chapter also involves connecting with other people, but for a different reason. Sometimes you just need to find someone who has more experience than you on something specific and get an answer, or at least their perspective. As a simple example, let's say you wake up one morning and you have a scary looking rash on your arm. You just need to know what it is, what caused it, and how to treat it. You wouldn't go to your mentor, because that person provides a different kind of guidance in your life. You wouldn't go to your network, because they might not want to hang around you and your strange arm rash. But you might ask the people in your network if they know a dermatologist.

In this case, you need a real expert—a medical professional who can help you. It is probably a one-time issue for you (let's hope). In this example you aren't looking to develop a relationship with the person beyond the doctor/patient kind, you simply need advice.

Let Me Ask Your Advice

In business it is often tactical advice you need. You have a problem or a question and the issue is usually time-bound. It might be something you have no idea how to do. It might be that you are having a problem with a coworker, boss, or customer. You need to get advice from someone who knows something about the subject. You are seeking a different perspective.

We tend to always think about the process of getting advice in a transaction where you ask and someone else responds. Most of the time that is probably true. But it can also occur in a more passive way. You might be involved in a conversation as a third party and listen as someone offers advice to someone else, and you file it away as something good to remember. Other times it may be something you read or a documentary you watched. Advice is all around us if we pay attention.

Sometimes people offer us advice and, at the time, we don't take it. For example, that happened to me when I worked for Walt Disney Company and was the editor in chief of the kid's magazine *Disney Adventures*. Disney had purchased a publication called *Family Fun*, which was created by a man named Jake. Jake was a very smart guy who had tremendous vision. He stayed on as the publisher but had a vision for what the internet was going to become. Way ahead of the times, he became one of the architects behind creating Disney.com. At that time in my career, I had a revolving door of bosses in a very short period. I briefly reported to Jake and my tenure with him was short, but it was terrific. He approached me and said he was looking for an editor in chief to run the new *Family Fun* website. This was back when websites were brand-new and groundbreaking. Interested in making a change, I threw my hat in the ring for that job and pitched my heart out for my candidacy. Jake came back to me and said he decided to hire someone else who had experience managing a high-profile consumer magazine website. Then he said, "Phyllis, I see you as somebody who has tremendous marketing and sales talent. Are you interested in being the director of marketing for this new venture reporting to the publisher?"

Disappointed at not getting the editor in chief role, my first reaction was that seemed like taking a step back. As a result, I didn't thoroughly consider it as the next logical career move for me at the time. I ended up leaving Disney on another track that catapulted me into cable television and has worked out well for me, but I will always question whether I should have taken that job.

If I had taken that fork in the road in the early days of the internet, where would my career be now? Could I have become an internet pioneer and made a gazillion dollars before the bubble burst? No regrets, but in retrospect, I should have listened more carefully to what Jake was saying to me. Ironically, my success post-Disney has been driven by the marketing and sales acumen that Jake accurately pointed out. When somebody tells you something that may be different from your own perspective, take the time to listen, explore the possibility, ask questions, and maybe seek others' opinions. Seek and consider advice instead of keeping it all inside yourself.

The University of the Internet

There are a lot of resources today beyond just your personal network. You can find advice for anything on the internet. A Google search will challenge you to wade through reams of information. YouTube is another bottomless resource. You can get direct advice in a video from someone you have never met. Remember that there are no tenured professors at this university, so consider the source, but you have more research at your fingertips than ever before in history.

There are so many places to go now for expert advice. For example, Joel and I were in Atlanta attending a formal charity event. Joel was wearing a tux and we could not figure out how to tie his bow tie in a way that looked sharp. Our efforts were turning out lousy, so we did what everyone does nowadays. We jumped on YouTube and the next thing we knew, Joel was ready to rock with the hippest crowd in Atlanta!

Know How to Ask

Self-awareness is a contributing factor to one's willingness and ability to ask for help. It takes humility to ask for help. Understand that no one is good at everything. Everyone needs to ask for help at some point. We often hesitate when asking for help, thinking we will be a burden by asking. If that describes you, consider using this self-test. The next time you hesitate to ask for advice, ask yourself, "Would I be willing to help someone else if they had the same question?" Chances are almost certain you would. It seems like more of a big deal to us than it probably will feel to that person.

Doing so might require you to come out of your comfort zone for half an hour. It does not require a permanent change. It might not seem like the kind of thing that requires practice, but the more you do it, the more comfortable you become. There is a considerable amount of research that shows people want to help other people as much as they can.[11] Often it comes down to how you ask. Be clear that you are considering options and you are not asking the person to make the decision for you. That takes some of the pressure off the other person. Change the nature of the question from "What do you think I should do?" to "If you were in my shoes, what would you do?"

Joel's Take

There are many benefits to asking for experts' advice. The first is the obvious one—you can get insights, information, suggestions, and other assistance to help you with whatever situation you are facing. The secondary benefit, and the one that stands out to me, is that by asking, you get noticed in a positive way. I think immediately of last semester when three students approached me after the first day of class. Tyanna, Ashley, and Jenny came up to me and introduced themselves. They told me that they had a great desire to learn a lot and participate in our class. They asked me what I would suggest they do to besides the assignments and asked if there was a way they could work with me to enhance their experience. They showed me how much they cared with enthusiasm and energy. I was impressed and made it a point to communicate with them regularly. They stood out. No doubt I spent more time with these students than with others, assisting with their projects, inviting them to seminars, opening doors to internships, and even sending them countless articles to read, above and beyond this specific class. Their final projects reflected the extra time they took to ask for help—both in the work necessary to score an A, but about careers, other classes, and life in general. As previously mentioned, I have spent a lifetime seeking out people smarter or more experienced than me. And as you might guess, it has paid off big time—for both them and me!

Be Specific

People are most comfortable offering advice when they are clear about what you are asking. Practice your question or jot it down to see if it is clear. The more specific you can be about what you are asking the person to help you with, the better. Understand exactly what you need advice about. Make people feel comfortable helping you. As a test, if, at the end of your request, is it possible the person might say, "Sure, I'm happy to help, but I'm not sure how to be helpful to you."? If so, your request is too vague.

Finally, think about the potential advice you might be able to offer in the future. Strong networks are reciprocal. What is it that you have that you can offer to help others?

Chapter Countdown
MAIN TAKEAWAYS FROM THIS CHAPTER:

- Valuable advice is all around you if you pay attention.
- Go to the right source for the kind of advice you need.
- Do your homework before you ask for advice.
- Be clear about what you are asking. Be concise and don't ramble. Write it out ahead of time if that helps.
- Advice is reciprocal. Be someone who is open and approachable when others need advice but also be careful about offering it if not asked.

CHAPTER 11
Work with Differences

If you are working in your first or second professional job, you have most likely already participated in company-sponsored diversity training of some kind. Those may have been in-person workshops or online training designed to take a deep dive into workplace issues like gender, racial, and other differences. The intent of this chapter is *not* to try to summarize all the evolving material that is out there on these subjects into a list of tips and tricks. Rather, it is a broader look at the ways to successfully work with people who are different from you—and who can help you throughout the course of your career.

Looking for Love in All the Wrong Places

The experience that caused me to change my perspective as well as some of my behavior in the workplace occurred when I was a senior level executive at Turner Broadcasting. I had the formative experience of attending a leadership development program at the Betsy Magness Leadership Institute, an executive leadership program for women in the cable and telecommunications industry.

During the first week of the program, we discussed many facets of leadership. We learned that it is vital for women to understand the psychology behind how women approach the workplace as compared to men. We got deep into a conversation about how many women have an unrealistic expectation that the workplace will be like a family. The impact of that mindset is that we tend to expect the same dynamics and the same behaviors as if we were at home interacting with our families. During that discussion, Lily, one of the course instructors, said something I'll never forget: "Don't be looking for love in all the wrong places." She wasn't talking about avoiding office romances. She channeled that old country western song as a warning to manage our expectations about the nature of the workplace.

There is also research that shows the sexes are more similar in their attitude toward work than they are different.[12] These studies show that differences are not rooted in gender traits. Rather, they are a result of company practices and structure that position men and women differently. While I respect the science behind those studies, the discussion in that room full of twenty-eight senior-level women was clear. As a female leader, it is important you understand that you can't take everything personally. That was one of my Achilles heels earlier in my career. I expected everybody to be loving, caring, and to go out of their way to get along and create a positive workplace. When it didn't work out that way, I would take it personally and be emotionally crushed. At some point a light bulb went off that work wasn't family, and it required a different mindset to be effective. From that moment on, I took challenging situations less personally and stopped wearing my heart on my sleeve. It's business. That doesn't mean I stopped caring for and supporting my coworkers. It just meant that I had to look at the work environment through a different lens.

And, while understanding that women and men may operate differently in the workplace, numerous men have been some of my biggest career champions and confidantes. Too numerous to mention (but you know who you are), I appreciate this opportunity to say a heartfelt THANK YOU to every one of them (of course, with Joel topping the list).

Working with (Your) Differences

So many times, when we think about differences, we think about race, gender, nationality, or other demographic differences. I believe that one of the most important aspects of working across differences is being aware of our own personality traits and accepting of others' traits. If you have ever taken one of the popular personality indicators like the Myers-Briggs Type Indicator or the WorkPlace Big Five, you already know that work teams are made up of people who are across the board when it comes to personality type. It is one of the things that makes life fun but can become a limiting factor if you expect everyone to be just like you. As I mentioned in Chapter 4, the self-awareness required to be clear on your own personality factors is one of the most important aspects of leadership.

Knowing our own personalities helps us understand what it might look like to stretch outside of our own comfort zone. Doing so helps us connect with people who are different than we are, and it also might help others see us in a different light. It reminds me of a time when I think doing so was a boost for my own career.

Years ago, I was working at Turner Broadcasting, and we were broadcasting the NBA All-Star game that year in Washington, DC. The whole Turner team was invited to attend a late night after-party. Normally I might have passed on a social event after a long workday, but Joel strongly suggested we go. It turned out to be the right decision. Turner used the event to entertain clients as well as an opportunity to celebrate a successful high-profile accomplishment. It gave us a chance to see our coworkers in a different context, meet their spouses and partners, and relax. I don't know for certain, but it may have been one of the reasons for my promotion to senior vice president sometime after that event. Senior people, including the president of Turner Sports, saw me as comfortable—and fun—in that environment.

That's a pretty glitzy example, but the reality is that we all have opportunities all of the time to push ourselves outside our comfort zone in ways that show us in a different light. Most large organizations have affinity groups of all kinds. Go to their events when you can, attend their meetings if invited, look for ways to try something you normally wouldn't do to see things from their perspective. One of the things I have learned is that so many times when an event is approaching, we think, "Oh I don't really feel up to doing that now. I think I'll just skip it." Here's a trick—don't let yourself dwell on how you feel now. Think about how you will feel after you go. And who knows, you might just have fun.

Listen to Your Mother

Okay, I'm not your mother. But I'll bet if she was here, she might say something like, "You're wearing *that* to your company's holiday party?" You know where I'm going next. You can and should be yourself, but my hope is that a big part of who you are as a person is someone with a professional sensitivity. While this chapter is about working across differences, it feels like a good place to remind everybody that you should be careful about pushing yourself to get out of your comfort zone and crossing the line in a way that would reflect on you unprofessionally whether you are male or female. In addition to dressing appropriately, your mom would suggest:

- Manage alcohol consumption.
- Remember that your behavior reflects on your organization (and your team, and your boss . . .).
- Get around, and connect with everyone, don't only stick with your clique.
- Don't gossip about coworkers.
- If there's karaoke, don't attempt any Britney Spears songs.

Generational Differences

There are at least four generations currently in the workplace, and there is a lot of popular thinking that says they are all vastly different. If you summarized these generalized differences and constructed a chart where everyone fits into a tidy little box based on the year they were born, it might look something like this.[13] [14]

	Baby Boomers	Gen X	Millennials/ Gen Y	Gen Z
Year born	1943-1960	1961-1980	1981-1996	1997-2010
Aspiration	Job security	Work-life balance	Freedom and flexibility	Security and stability
Career attitude	Organizational. Careers defined by employers	Loyalty to profession, not employer	Digital entrepreneurs, work with, not for, organizations	Career multitaskers, move between organizations and gigs.
Positive stereotypes	Committed to the organization. Good team players, mentors.	Committed to diversity, being global, juggling work and family. Biggest revenue producers.	Tenacious. Adaptive. Team player, can relate to anybody.	Tech competent. Entrepreneurial. Always on.
Negative stereotypes	Judgmental. Out of touch. Dogmatic	Cynical. Poor team member	Entitled. Lazy.	Cynical and not loyal

I'm not going to argue about the fact that there are differences across these different groups. But I have always believed that people have more in common than they have differences. Turns out I was right—partly. An article in *Harvard Business Review* states that differences solely based on generation alone are not valid.[15] Their research indicates that what makes the most differences are when people's *beliefs* are different. These age-related stereotypes, however, may affect how people think about and treat each other.

Other factors attributed to these behaviors are not so much about the generation as a personality type but more relative to where people are in their career. In other words, it wouldn't surprise me that a senior vice president colleague of mine might not be interested in changing jobs every couple of years, just considering where she is in her career and life cycle.

I have had the good fortune to work with ambitious, personable, and trusted colleagues from every generation. My strategy has been to talk honestly about these generational stereotypes, show respect and learn from all generational groups, and focus on the team's goals and values together.

Chapter Countdown

MAIN TAKEAWAYS FROM THIS CHAPTER:

- People have more in common than they have differences.
- Don't take everything personally. It's not about you.
- Generational differences have frequently been overstated.
- Attend events you normally wouldn't.
- Seek out organizational affinity groups.

3
Section

NAVIGATE YOUR
COURSE

CHAPTER 12

Be Realistic, Be Resilient, Be Relentless

This chapter tackles the personal issues and challenges of being a woman as you build your career. It is for those of you who might be trying to manage a career and have a family or are just simply trying to manage the integration of your personal and professional lives. We all have personal demands that, as women, add pressure to the rocketing of our potential.

Be Realistic

I have always thought that the starting point for planning anything is being willing to face the facts of any situation objectively. There are many things that can impact your career trajectory that are not in your control. Let's take, for one example, the impact that the COVID-19 pandemic had on women in the workplace. It's not a pretty picture.

One reason that working women were under increased pressure during the pandemic was due to the continuing gender disparity in roles. For example, let's say that your childcare coverage fell through for some reason on a given day. In so many cases, when it comes down to who will stay home with the children, it's mom. There is understandable concern that all the progress gained in recent years supporting women rising in the workplace, having a voice, and being more represented in the C-suite took a step back during COVID-19. This is backed up by research, according to a 2021 McKinsey report,

> At the beginning of 2020, the representation of women in corporate America was trending—albeit slowly—in the right direction. Between January 2015 and December 2019, the number of women in senior-vice-president positions increased from 23 to 28 percent, and in the C-suite from 17 to 21 percent. But COVID-19 dealt a major setback.

The pandemic had a near-immediate effect on women's employment. One in four women are considering leaving the workforce or downshifting their careers versus one in five men.[16]

That information caught my attention because I saw it playing out in the places I have worked. What came next in the report is particularly disturbing.

> While all women have been impacted, three major groups have experienced some of the largest challenges: working mothers, women in senior management positions, and Black women. This disparity came across as particularly stark with parents of kids under ten: the rate at which women in this group were considering leaving was ten percentage points higher than for men.[17]

For all we talk about sharing the load at home, the reality is that in many cases, women are largely in charge of family care. Of course, this isn't everyone's situation, and many families manage to share these responsibilities equally. The research, however, says that most haven't. My point here is that to create a plan for your trajectory, there are realities that we all face, and we should do so with our eyes wide open. What should readers take from this? If you want to have a family, have parents that need your attention, or have other passions outside of work, you're going to have to figure out how you juggle it all. My experience has been that I've had to make sacrifices along the way and that I've had to make tough choices on what was more important to me at a moment. Don't get me wrong—I went after what I wanted and didn't want to compromise, but I had to be realistic.

Be Aware of Your Priorities

As you build your career and grow your personal life, it comes down to having clarity about your priorities. If you're at the beginning of your career, you are preparing for blastoff. At that point, what are your priorities? Do they involve being focused on getting established in your career and getting more clarity on your career path? Or are you more focused on your relationships and have decided that you want to have a family sooner rather than later? It comes down to figuring out what you want your life plan to be and then being realistic about how you're going to get there.

It is easy to get caught up in the popular messaging that "You can have it all." That sounds great, but it is a bit unrealistic to think anyone can have everything in all aspects of their life all at one time. You can achieve a lot, but you must be open to the tradeoffs. One mistake a lot of women make is not carving out any time or room to take care of themselves. You must pay attention to your own physical, emotional, and even spiritual well-being because nobody else is going to do it for you.

Stuff Happens

A critical part of being realistic is being prepared for and thoughtful about the tradeoffs that we invariably must make at certain times. It's like the bumper sticker says, "Shit Happens." My experience is that the more realistic we are, the less we are thrown off course when life intervenes with our plans. For me, this means being clear about my expectations.

When Joel and I got married, we became a blended family. We worked hard at home to help Joel's children, Jennifer and Jonathan, merge with my son Andrew into a new family structure and environment. At the same time, Joel and I had demanding corporate jobs. I naïvely thought that love conquers all and we would immediately become one happy family. Trust me, we were not! Working my tail off trying to build my career while building a "normal" family environment at home almost pushed me to the breaking point. In retrospect, I wasn't at all realistic about the combined demands and sacrifices that would be required. As we approached a crisis point, we took stock of the reality. We had to admit to ourselves that things weren't going the way we hoped and that we were going to have to make some immediate and significant sacrifices.

"Phyllis, you need to get your house in order and put your career on a back burner right now," was the sobering advice from our family therapist at the time. My decision was to put my new family first and go into career "orbit." I made the difficult decision to leave my corporate job and take on select freelance jobs under the umbrella of my own communications company until things were in a better place. I have never regretted the decision, which led to my next career adventure at Disney a year later. To this day, having a "modular family," coined by our current family therapist from whom we still seek advice from time to time, can still be challenging.

A Surprising Key to Happiness

There is so much information out there shouting at us to "have it all" that we start to believe that is the path we should all be following. If you look closely, much of the shouting is marketing hoopla to sell us something. It turns out having it all (or trying to) doesn't necessarily make us happier. Instead, being realistic about your expectations turns out to be a huge factor in your overall happiness. According to Barry Schwartz, a psychologist and author of *The Paradox of Choice: Why More is Less*, the secret to happiness is having low expectations.

Wait, what?

Before you decide that must be the gloomiest advice ever, consider Schwartz's premise. His research has shown that an overwhelming set of options available to us living in modern Western societies increases our expectations that there is one perfect choice.[18] In his TED Talk on the subject he describes a trip to his neighborhood grocery store where he counted an astounding 175 different types of salad dressing.[19] This increased his expectation that, with all those choices, there must be one perfect salad dressing for you—if only you make the right choice. And, as Schwartz points out, no salad dressing is perfect. As a result, when you get home and taste the salad dressing you buy—after spending way too much time in the salad dressing aisle—you are likely to be unhappy with your choice and probably your lunch.

His point is that as choices increase, it raises your expectations and reduces the chance that you will ever be pleasantly surprised. The best you can hope for is that something is as a good as you expected. In other words, adequate. What about you? When was the last time you were "pleasantly surprised"? What Schwartz is suggesting is that lowering our expectations (that are often set with little data) can fill our lives with pleasant surprises and increase the happiness we feel when that happens.

It turns out there is research that backs Schwartz up. Neuroscientists at University College London agree that avoiding high expectations really is the key to happiness. The researchers also found that the participants' happiness depended not on how they were doing compared to others, but on whether they were doing better than they had expected.[20]

Those are two gold nuggets that we can all use. First, keep expectations reasonable and learn to appreciate being pleasantly surprised. Second, don't build your happiness by comparing your accomplishments to other people. Instead, become more aware of exceeding your own expectations for yourself.

Be aware of, and thoughtful about, the tradeoffs that you invariably must make. "I want it all" is a nice idea, but what is realistic is different for everyone. My take on this is not to put unnecessary pressure on yourself. It's perfectly fine to have big goals and want to be known as a high performer as long as you manage your own expectations along the way. Very often we are our harshest critic.

Be Resilient

So even if you have realistic expectations, what do you do when "shit happens"?

Sometimes you can continue to stay on your career trajectory and soar ahead, and other times you might have to temporarily put your career into orbit. Things happen in all our lives that we don't anticipate, and that's when resilience becomes critical. Like so many things we talk about in this book, it takes us back to the importance of self-awareness and understanding your core values. At the end of the day, it's great to have a good job and a promising career, but it's only one piece of our whole life pie.

There's no right or wrong here. The main thing is to consider interruptions in your forward career progress as interruptions rather than end points. Finding the right answer for yourself when "shit happens" is an important part of finding your own path. Drop back, reassess, revisit your goals, alter course, but never give up.

Be Relentless

I don't know anyone whose career trajectory has been a perfect straight line. Most people I have worked with have all had setbacks. Some were small, and some were huge. But the people who successfully navigated setbacks have some things in common. I have already mentioned the first two—the ability and willingness to be realistic and resilient. The third key factor is that no matter what, they didn't give up. They kept plugging ahead. They may have taken time to lick their wounds and possibly reassess their goals, but they kept moving. They eventually bounced back—and frequently ended up in a better situation than before.

When I worked at both Disney and Turner Broadcasting, I observed corporate politics that often resulted in turmoil and senior-level executives being blindsided and ousted from their roles. This happened to one of my mentors at Turner Broadcasting, a high-level talented and well-liked executive. What he did at that point was to take a step back, lick his wounds, and take a realistic look at what he should do next. He was humble enough to analyze what had happened and figure out another scenario that he could put into play. It might not involve immediately jumping back into a high executive-level job, but that didn't matter at that moment. He was willing to roll up his sleeves, take some risks, and reach out to his contacts and lean on his extensive relationships to help guide him through this setback.

His journey back was by no means a straight line, but to fast-forward in this story, he eventually worked his way up to become one of the highest and most respected executives in the media and communications business today.

His is a great example of incorporating all three of the Rs throughout one's career journey by being realistic, resilient, and relentless.

Chapter Countdown
MAIN TAKEAWAYS FROM THIS CHAPTER:

- Traditional gender roles are still in place.
- Clarity on your personal and professional priorities can help you avoid the "you can have it all" trap.
- One key to being happier is the management of your expectations.
- Look to others for inspiration but not comparison.
- Career trajectory is seldom a straight line.

CHAPTER 13
Embrace Change and Hang on Tight

Much of what I have talked about so far in this book is the need to be flexible and resilient. There is a reason for that, and the reason is that the only thing that's constant in the world of work and life is change. There are so many examples, particularly in technology, about how fast the world is moving. Change or die. That phrase was made famous by author Alan Deutschman when he wrote about it in a *Fast Company* cover story.[21] He points out how difficult it is for human beings to change, even when their lives depend on it. Deutschman isn't the first to connect the need to change with survival. Charles Darwin and others before him demonstrated how change occurs in nature and how living creatures evolve to survive.

The Constancy of Change

Throughout my career, I have certainly had to continually adapt. Sometimes it was easy, but most of the time it was a challenge. I have worked for companies that were sold to another company, merged with another company, or reorganized seemingly annually. Along with all of that came a revolving roster of bosses.

Then there are the changes that, on the surface, don't seem to be that big in retrospect, but at the time were quite disruptive. In my very first job as an editorial assistant at *American Baby* magazine, I remember the day they announced we were getting brand-new computers. I guess that dates me a bit. It was a stretch to adjust to it, but it was a quantum leap for the better—once I adjusted to it. And that is the key. Change often looks like a problem before we have given it a chance. When that happened, my parents gave me a framed poster of an old-fashioned typewriter by an artist named Anne Laddon. I'm sitting here in my office today, thirty years later, looking at that poster. I have taken it with me in every job that I've had to remind me of where I started and the positive possibilities of change.

The advent of personal computers wasn't the only change at *American Baby*. When I started there, it was a small family business owned by two cousins. In some ways it was an idyllic first job in a small company with a family atmosphere. I could walk down the hallway to one of the owners and say, "I have an idea to bounce off of you." They would listen and respond, and we would work together to determine if the idea had possibilities. It gave me the incredible opportunity at an early stage in my career to be an idea generator and executor. They eventually sold the business to a huge corporation called Cahners Publishing, one of the largest publishers of trade magazines in the US (later acquired by an even larger global company called Reed Elsevier).

We had to adjust from working in a tight-knit family culture to a conglomerate in which we were just one small piece. That was a huge change and a big cultural transition. The change brought with it a formal executive board and annual business planning process. There was also an annual editorial review process and for the first time, my work was evaluated by a creative advisor. Although intimidating at first, I learned a great deal from him, especially how to write compelling magazine cover lines. I also learned that text with all capital letters is hard to read—an enduring golden rule for all sales presentations and materials my team produces today.

The Impact of Change Role Models

I like to think that I have managed change well over my career. One reason is that I saw this modeled impressively by my parents. They owned the family toy and sporting goods business, Rugby Sport Shop in Brooklyn, for many years. Then, in their fifties, they sold the business and moved to Florida. Things in their lives were changing. The economic strength of the neighborhood was in decline and the rigors of a seven-days-a-week retail business were taking their toll. As a result, they had to figure out what they were going to do next. After growing up in the family business (his bedroom was literally in the back of the store) and later acquiring the family business, I watched my dad subsequently reinvent himself. He built a thirty-five-year career as a financial planner with Raymond James. He retired as an assistant vice president when he was eighty-eight years old and still checked the stock market every day until he passed away just shy of his ninety-third birthday. Mom, a former bookkeeper before helping Dad run the store, became his trusted partner. She was a tremendous asset with clients and helped impeccably plan educational luncheons for prospective and current clients at local restaurants.

From an early age it gave me some perspective to be able to sit back and say, "Well, my parents are being open to the reality of the changes around them and are adapting and surviving. They're moving on with their careers." By comparison, I also saw other people doing the opposite. They saw themselves as the victims of change and whined and complained and refused to get with the program. I was able to see that things weren't going so well for them. I think I realized that, whether I liked it or not, if I wanted to remain in a company where I was, or in a job where I was, that I was going to have to be flexible and be open about changing. It definitely helped me to ride the ups and downs that come with the corporate change that we can't avoid.

Important Lessons for Future Leaders

All the many, many changes also informed how I wanted to treat the people who worked for me when things were changing. For those of you with direct reports or project team members, it is a good exercise to consider your own reactions to change and how you can make things better for others.

First, clearly describe what is not changing. It is important for people to know the extent of the changes right away, and one way to do that is to be clear about what is staying the same. Your audience will appreciate having something to hold on to. Second, get people comfortable with what the vision is and why change is occurring. It is important to build a value proposition in a plan that shows why and how this change will lead to improvement and, of course, *what's in it for them*. You always must look through the lens of the person who might be resisting the change. How can you make them feel included, empowered, and involved in helping to navigate that change? For people who are just naturally resistant to change or have a hard time with it, find out why it makes them anxious and uncomfortable. Shine a light on the tension rather than ignoring it. Give people an opportunity to share their reactions and listen to their fears that they think the change will introduce.

Joel's Take

To function in any business environment, you must accept the fact that there will be change. It's inevitable, and one needs to get ahead of the curve by focusing beyond their immediate job. This involves knowing where the organization is going and what is happening in the world you and your customers are experiencing. And I believe that some portion of that learning needs to go on *outside* of the environment of your current employer. And even your work group's function. This could include meetings with a wider variety of people in your organization to broaden your perspective about your company's business. It should also include looking outside of your organization and keeping up with changes in the world and marketplace. You can do this by subscribing to blogs, joining your field's professional society, following relevant TED Talks, taking a course, or just talking to people and getting ahead of the curve a bit.

It's all a method of keeping current in a way that will help you anticipate change so that it doesn't come as a surprise. Better yet, you will be better positioned to deal with it when it does occur. An example might be understanding that most decisions made in business are data-driven. Hence, make sure you understand the role of data mining and the tools needed to analyze that data. Learn the various research companies and what they offer. Access trend reports and learn what the experts are saying about the future.

Too many people receive change with a victim mindset. Change is going to happen. There are things you can be doing now to deal with it and even come out of it ahead of the game.

The Hang on Tight Part

Change is so inevitable that if you don't think you can deal with change, then you need to really think about what kind of career you're going into. There are some careers that are less impacted by potential change. Even better than that, when change is unescapable, flip it in your mind and say, "Okay, what's the opportunity here? How can I capitalize on the opportunity and how can I get comfortable with being uncomfortable?"

The reason I titled this chapter "Embrace Change and Hang on Tight" is because I like the metaphor of change being like riding a roller coaster. As a kid growing up in Brooklyn, my first roller coaster experience was on the iconic and appropriately named Coney Island Cyclone, the second steepest wooden roller coaster in the world. The big, bad coaster was terrifying, and I closed my eyes, screamed, and held on for dear life. To this day, I may not like roller coasters, but if I hang on tight, I can make it through. It's going to be scary, and I'm going to be white-knuckled the whole time. But—I can do it. And when it's over, I will have made it through, having had a shared experience with others that probably brought us together a bit. Not only that, but the next time I ride the roller coaster, I might not have white knuckles at all. It just takes some courage to sit down in the seat and let them drop that bar over your lap.

Chapter Countdown

MAIN TAKEAWAYS FROM THIS CHAPTER:

- Change is reality—learn to be adaptable.
- Most people interpret change as a problem.
- Observing how your role models deal with change is highly instructional.
- Understand that you can make change easier for others by seeing the event through their eyes.
- Expect change and hang on tight until that roller coaster ride ends.

CHAPTER 14

Build Consensus from the Top Down and the Bottom Up

One of the keys to long-lasting professional (and personal) success is learning how to build consensus. Consensus has many definitions, but my favorite is: working toward solutions that are best for everyone, not just best for you. Most often consensus is used to decide or resolve something. But more than that, arriving at consensus should not only move the group forward, but it should also strengthen the relationships of the group members. This aspect often gets overlooked if we are plowing forward to a decision. In fact, sometimes relationships are damaged when reaching consensus is done the wrong way.

Most of us are more experienced at building consensus than we realize. Building consensus isn't something that just begins when you have a job. If you think about it, it is likely that it started when you were young. You probably had to try to build consensus with groups of friends, family members, teammates, or other members of groups.

Consensus Is Not the Same as Majority Rules

Consensus is often confused with taking a vote. I have heard people say things like, "Okay, the vote is eight to five, so we have a consensus, let's move ahead with the plan." Well, no, you have not reached a consensus. You have voted. Having a vote is easier and faster in most cases, but it is less desirable because:

- Voting can lead to division and competition within the group.
- Voting does not allow for compromise; it is your way or my way. There is no middle option.
- Voting creates winners and losers. In the example above, even after taking a vote and moving ahead, you still have five people opposed.
- Voting doesn't offer a way to start from common ground.

Consensus is about collaboration and cooperation and a genuine desire to listen to everyone's opinions to reach an agreement. When done well, a decision by consensus leaves the person most opposed saying something like, "Well, it wouldn't be my first choice, but I can live with what we have decided as a group."

If you learn how to build consensus among the people you work with—from your boss and direct reports to peers and junior colleagues—you will increase your effectiveness and strengthen your personal brand.

Treat Everyone at All Levels with Respect

Building consensus starts before any meeting or decision must be made. It starts with how you treat people on a day-to-day basis. One common mistake people make is focusing on building relationships solely from the top down, starting with senior management. If you work in a company with many internal stakeholders, it's critical to develop relationships at all levels. Sometimes that begins with a junior team member or assistant. In fact, executive assistants can be highly influential. Throughout the years, I have always asked my assistants how others treat them. If I hear good things, I am apt to go out of my way for those individuals. If people are rude or dismissive to lower-level staff members, that can become a problematic part of their personal brand.

You never know when former colleagues may reappear in your life. Coincidentally, a year ago, two talented former Time Warner colleagues joined our Spectrum Reach team—one as our new chief marketing officer and the other as an executive assistant, both reporting to our president. Fortunately, my previous relationships with both were built on collaboration and mutual respect. The Golden Rule of "treat others as you want to be treated" applies to everyone in the business world as well.

Joel's Take

Effective consensus building is based on trust. People must be able to trust that you are being forthcoming, honest, and genuine with them, even if it doesn't support your personal position. That process of being trusted starts early in your work relationships. It's almost as if we have labels on our forehead that describe us—and what is written on those labels is a result of our past behaviors.

What do you want your label to say? To increase your effectiveness as a consensus builder, ideally it would say something like, "I respect everyone in this organization, no matter what level position they hold." You don't want your label to say something like, "I only respect the people in the organization who I believe are in a position to help me get what I want." Whether you are dealing with somebody's assistant or the janitor or a new employee you need to be the person who can and does provide some degree of connection and support and sees things from the other person's perspective.

Your label becomes your brand, and you want your brand to stand for something. People pick up on your sincerity and whether you really are concerned about their well-being. In an ideal world you would be treating people in a way that builds their trust in you. That way, when it comes time to build consensus, you can lead from a position of trust that you have already established. Getting to consensus can be hard enough, but it can be almost impossible if people don't trust that you have everyone's best interest in mind—not just your own.

Talk Less, Listen More

One of the guiding principles of building consensus is to listen. Everyone likes to be heard. When you are charged with developing new projects or ideas, seek the opinions of others, and listen to their advice. Talk to the people who are closest to the business. For example, eleven years ago, my first mission at Time Warner Cable Media was to transform a marketing team to better serve the changing needs of the business and clients in more than twenty-five markets across the East. The foundation of my ninety-day plan was a listening tour visiting as many markets as possible to hear directly from sales team members and cross-functional partners at all levels. I would never have been able to develop a successful plan from our corporate headquarters in New York without that intelligence. Of course, today we are all learning to also make those vital connections virtually, but the same principles apply.

Collaborate with Colleagues

Before an important meeting or discussion, it's a good idea to solicit input from key internal stakeholders—but not to fortify your own position or maneuver behind the scenes for backup. Instead, consider it an opportunity to better understand other perspectives besides your own. This approach proved especially productive when I spearheaded a complex initiative with a working project team of more than fifty colleagues. In advance of every update with the president of our division, I briefed my boss and other meeting attendees on my recommendations and asked for feedback to ensure alignment at the meeting. You can also practice this approach with colleagues on any simple assignment or project you take on, even planning a team morale-building outing or surprise birthday celebration for your boss.

Empower and Acknowledge Your Team

As mentioned earlier, building consensus is anchored in trust. Look for ways to recognize people before you ever need to build consensus. If—or when—you manage people, you will find that it is important to make them feel empowered and appreciated. When someone on your team does a great job, acknowledge the contribution and share it with other managers and your boss. A heartfelt "Thank you" or "Well done!" can go a long way. When people on your team shine, you shine even brighter! Always remember that people who report to you can spread the word about whether they think you're a supportive boss or a difficult boss—both inside and outside your company.

Take advantage of company employee rewards programs to congratulate team members in other departments. At Spectrum Reach, we have a great program called Spark. Every month we celebrate team members who have both received and given Spark awards.

Ultimately, building consensus "top down" and "bottom up" is about trust. When you succeed at earning that trust, you will be poised for sustained success.

Chapter Countdown
MAIN TAKEAWAYS FROM THIS CHAPTER:

- Building consensus starts with the way you treat people before you have to start building consensus.
- Provide everyone with all the information available before trying to build consensus.
- Trust is the foundation of consensus.
- Consensus does not mean taking a vote.
- A critical catalyst for consensus is listening.

CHAPTER 15
Manage Your Boss

You might look at the title of this chapter and say, "Hey, wait a minute. Why is it my responsibility to manage my boss?" My answer to that is, to have the most optimal experience and to forge the best relationship and the best outcomes for yourself, there are a few things you must figure out. How can you forge a strong bond with your boss in a professional and helpful way? How can you make their life easier? How can you best work within your boss's personality type and management style to be effective? Every boss is different, and it is up to you to put in the work to figure this out.

I Can See a Good Meeting in Your Future

One of the keys to success with bosses is to be like a psychic and be able to "read the tea leaves." This means being aware of your boss's current mindset *in the moment*. For example, if you have a one-on-one meeting with your boss, you may have your own agenda and some things you want to accomplish. You must be savvy enough to read your boss's mood that day. I start every one-one-one meeting with my boss with a question: "How are you doing?" Their answer can be very telling. For example, your boss may have just left a frustrating meeting with their boss, had a negative experience with a key client, or is just under the weather that day. This is probably not the right time to pitch a new idea or lobby for additional hires for your group. Of course, it's easier to read body language and facial expressions when you are able meet in person. If your boss is in a different location or if you are connecting virtually, you may have some additional challenges.

I'm not suggesting that you walk around your boss on eggshells. Sometimes to drive the best outcomes in that relationship, you must be sensitive and know when the time is right, and you have your boss's full attention and energy for engaging with you and your ideas. I've had many situations where I went in with my own agenda and came out accomplishing nothing on that agenda because my boss had *their* own agenda. Or, I read the room and the mood said, "Hm, today's not a good day to go for that. I'm going to hold off on that until another time and another meeting." Just as I start every one-on-one meeting with a question, I end with a question: "Is there anything else you need from me?"

Getting to Know Your Boss's Style and Preferences

Understanding how your boss thinks and operates requires that you pay attention to their personality and work style. Are they introverted or extroverted? Do they like to get lots of details from you, or do they just like the headlines? Do they want to be copied on everything or would they resent you overloading their email box? Would they rather have a phone conversation or an in-person conversation instead of email or text? Do they like short, pithy reports, or do they really prefer lot of facts and data? Those are things you need to understand in terms of how much to offer up or not offer up.

Joel's Take

Bosses are people too. They have issues, challenges, and pressures. Recognizing and understanding your boss's viewpoint is of utmost importance. We often place bosses on a pedestal that at times gives us an inaccurate view of their daily functions and daily issues. Our job is to make

bosses look good and ease their burden. You need to make an effort to be in touch with their style and get into their "comfort zone." For example, three of my career stops came with bosses who had completely different styles.

John was old school, by the book, and relied on a lifetime of his experience to make every decision. To work well with him, I always came prepared, with lots of data to support my recommendations and ideas. I respected his time, even dressed more formally, and honored his experience and seniority.

Jerry, on the other hand was a creative thinker with an entrepreneurial spirit. He was super smart and often made decisions based on gut. With Jerry I listened, listened, and listened more. He liked to talk, pontificate, and riff—like a jazz musician. It was like dancing or playing in a band with Jerry—you had to be ready to shake and bake. You might guess—casual attire was appropriate and bringing fun snacks for brainstorming sessions was always a good idea.

Paul was a super bright, self-made executive who started out writing a fanzine about the comics industry, the characters, and the storylines. A world-recognized expert on superheroes, he came from the creative and editorial side of the business, not sales and marketing. I had to understand how he perceived sales and adjust my style while opening his eyes to the benefits of sales and marketing. To gain his respect, I had to show him that I understood, respected, and honored the legacy of these superhero characters. My job was to prove to him that there was a way to sell, market, and exploit these characters with class and dignity while generating lucrative licensing fees. Paul was more conservative than Jerry, requiring a different tone until he got to know, like, and respect me. Thankfully, my insight, patience, and hard work paid off.

Three uber successful bosses, three totally different styles that I had to match up with. And I did. Guess that acting background paid off!

You Are Here

I've had back-to-back bosses who were the exact opposite of each other in the same role and had to adjust my behavior 180 degrees going from one to the next. When I first started with Time Warner Cable Media eleven years ago, the person who hired me (and was my boss) was based in Charlotte, North Carolina. Based in New York City, my charge was to quickly learn a completely new business to me—local cable television. Brought in to help lead a marketing team for the East region of the US, I inherited a team of people and would need to do a rapid reorganization.

I jumped in and started to learn the business. Throughout this time, my boss, Carole, was very busy and at times seemed overwhelmed. It was super difficult to get her on the phone and getting a meeting on her calendar was almost impossible. What was I going to do? First, I had to figure out how I was going to learn pieces of the business from other colleagues. And then, when I was able to get time with her and started sharing my plan for the initial reorganization, it just wasn't resonating. I learned that Carole was someone who always needed context. One of her favorite sayings was, "Let's pretend we're walking through the mall, and you see the mall map on the directory. It always has a little red circle that says, 'You are here.' When we have a meeting, I want to start with knowing where we are before you start telling me where you want to go."

To be successful in working with Carole, I had to speak her language. If I wanted to be understood, I always had to offer up context. I had to come in and lay out the table and say, okay, this is where we are today. This is the current situation. These are the recommendations for the future. And once I did that, we were able to forge a bond. We worked together for years, and both got promoted to bigger jobs. We supported and encouraged one another through a two-year merger roller coaster (remember the white knuckles). She retired after the merger, and we continue to have a tremendous fondness for one another that I would never have predicted with our rocky start. It speaks to the importance of understanding your boss's personality and work style—and then accommodating or getting in their comfort zone while still being true to yourself.

Just When You Think You Have It Figured Out

One of the reasons I initially had difficulty adjusting to the style of my first boss at Time Warner Cable Media is that my boss before her had such a different style. I worked for Jacquie, the CEO and founder of a start-up, who was a brilliant MBA from Columbia. She built her career in the banking industry in business process redesign—a drastically different field than marketing or media. She was a force of nature and was all about inductive thinking. Her style was almost the opposite of Carole's, which was know where you're starting and then figure out where you're going. Jacquie's approach was that you need to know the desired outcome of where you're going to end up. Then you can back up to a starting point. Going from one style to the other felt very abrupt to me and initially made my head spin. For example, if you were trying to close a new business deal, you had to predict how many meetings and interactions you would have and anticipate the reactions to each of those interactions from the prospective client. Once I fundamentally understood this critical step, it made managing my boss much easier for me.

No Monkeys Allowed

Another one of my former bosses gave me an article from the *Harvard Business Review* called "Who's Got the Monkey?"[22] It's an old article, but a classic. (I guess I'm not the only one who took it to heart, because it is still one of HBR's best-selling reprints.) In essence it means you always want to bring your boss possible solutions to problems. Don't be someone who just brings problems into your boss's office and puts that problem "monkey" on your boss's shoulders. Now your boss has one more problem to solve before you came in. How eager do you think the boss will be to see you coming toward their office if they suspect you will be unloading another monkey?

I give a copy of that article to every single person who works for me now. It doesn't mean that you always have the answers because sometimes we do need our boss to help us with problems, especially when we're more junior in our career. A good approach is to say, "I may need some help here, but here are some potential ideas and potential solutions." Bosses react a lot better to that than just feeling you're going to dump your monkey on their back. Problem solvers are the people who get promoted. One small change of perspective that is helpful is to reframe "problems" as "challenges." This always helps me reframe the context for developing solutions.

Help Your Boss Help You

Finally, one aspect of managing your boss is ensuring that your boss knows what you are doing. This might sound trite, but does your boss really know what you do on a daily basis? Do they know what you are good at, and what differentiates you from others? That doesn't mean that you email a blow-by-blow account of each day to your boss. It does mean that you have to take the lead in making sure that your boss has an accurate picture of your work. This is an aspect of communication that we often overlook. Or we avoid it because we don't want to appear to be blowing our own horn. Think of it as keeping your boss informed enough to describe to others the unique contributions you bring to the organization.

It is a bit of role reversal to consider managing your boss, but it is a critical aspect of creating a solid working relationship with your boss and making your own contributions visible.

Chapter Countdown
MAIN TAKEAWAYS FROM THIS CHAPTER:

- Bosses are people too. They are often overwhelmed with their own challenges. How can you help them?
- Bosses can differ wildly from each other. Anticipate this and be adaptable to different styles.
- Understand your boss's communication preferences and style.
- Avoid dumping your monkeys onto your boss's back.
- Do not assume that your boss has an accurate picture of your work and your results.

CHAPTER 16
Get a Thumbs-Up for a Heads-Up

One of the first lessons we learn is the massive importance of effective communication at work. The problem is, this is such a wide sweeping subject. Any suggestion from me like, "Be a good communicator" is so general that it isn't helpful. Plus, you already know communication is critical. That's why I focus this chapter on one very specific and important aspect of communication—the art of the "heads-up."

Caught Off Guard

Recently I encountered a situation that reminded me of one of the potential communication pitfalls that, unfortunately, is all too common. During a late afternoon group leadership video call, I was caught off guard when I learned about a human resources departmental reorganization that was going to significantly impact my team and me. Without any input or advance notice, I found out in the meeting that some of my most trusted and favorite human resources business partners were no longer going to support recruiting and personnel issues for me. My heart sank, and I could feel the blood rushing to my face. I could barely contain my surprise and initial disappointment, which was quickly followed by anger. Since this was a video meeting, I knew that my reaction was on display for everyone. The rest of the half-hour call seemed interminable.

After the meeting ended, I immediately picked up the phone and confronted my key department partner to express my initial concerns. For weeks I had been asking for clarity and was coyly told that news was coming soon. I told him I felt blindsided by him sharing the news in a group setting. He reassured me that my team was being given additional support and that my trusted human resources business partners would still be able to lean in as needed. After thinking about it overnight, what really bothered me was the total lack of advance warning from my colleague—no heads-up. How could a close colleague for the last ten years not inform me about the announcement and the changes he knew would be a significant change in personnel supporting my team?

The Benefit of Hindsight

In retrospect, I should have taken the time to reflect on and absorb the news before reacting so quickly by jumping on the phone. In most cases, acting or reacting too quickly to surprising news or changes is not a wise idea. Often our emotions drive our first response, and until we process the emotions, we cannot arrive at logic, which is usually the better position to create our response

The next morning, I scheduled time with my colleague to clear the air and continue the conversation. I told him that if he had just taken the time to reach out to me before the group call, we could have avoided a very awkward and very public incident. It would have reinforced our trust as well as given me time to privately process the news. I also realized that my colleague had a new boss, and whether he agreed with the plan, he had to publicly support it. With that in mind, I told him I would do my best to make it work—and did. As a result, my relationship with this colleague got back on a strong track. Months later some additional personnel shifts were made that granted my original requests and have ended up being great for my team.

If It Happens to You

If this has ever happened to you, I'm sure you remember it vividly. If it has not, it is only a matter of time. Take a deep breath and look at the situation from both or even multiple points of view. Even though in the moment you might have felt caught off guard or like someone sprung a trap, consider— just consider—that maybe that was not the person's intent. Is it possible that it was an honest mistake? If so, if your reaction is to immediately flame back, you could be causing severe damage to your reputation and your work relationships.

One way to think of it is this: "After I work through whatever emotional reaction I am having from this incident, I am going to have a private follow-up conversation to give that person a chance to explain what happened in the meeting from their perspective. I will withhold my reaction until I learn more."

That doesn't mean that you won't stick up for yourself or become a door mat. It just means that you will sequence your reactions differently.

Joel's Take

Giving a heads-up works both ways. I never want to be the one that catches someone off guard. I have a rule that one should never assume anything in communication. I find that so often we make assumptions that we know what people think and believe. We assume we know what information they already have, and we even assume we know how people feel about us. This assumption can lead to misunderstandings at best—and big, big problems at worst. As human beings we have the opportunity to be sensitive to other people by putting ourselves into their shoes and seeing the world from their perspective. Much of the time it is as simple as following the Golden Rule. How would you like people to communicate with you? You probably want people to communicate with you professionally, honestly, and completely.

I have tried to make it a habit of never assuming that someone already knows all they need to know. That means that I must intentionally connect with people before an important meeting. It means that I must always keep everyone on my team in the loop. It also means that I should never assume the people close to me know how much I love them. These are all examples of how avoiding assumptions in communication has helped me be more effective as well as maintaining and improving my relationships with people.

I believe that the relationships we have in organizations are at the core of our daily work lives. And because we spend more time at work than anything else (other than sleeping), I believe in the power of quality and quantity of communication. I want others to have the right information they need, and because I don't want to assume I know what they know, I would much rather over-communicate then under-communicate.

Clear the Air

One-on-one conversations (not email or texts) go a long way to build and strengthen business relationships. They are especially important as many of us work more virtually and need to make a concerted effort to stay connected with key colleagues and partners. It is truly amazing how much power you have in guiding the narrative with your colleagues by *thinking first* and coming up with a strategy to address potential conflicts. The result is most gratifying to say the least.

And don't forget, you can use the same approach in your personal life to strengthen important relationships with family and friends.

Chapter Countdown

MAIN TAKEAWAYS FROM THIS CHAPTER:

- Think ahead and over-communicate—if necessary—to prevent catching someone off guard.
- How you handle yourself when that happens to you is critical. It is understandable to have an emotional reaction first, and you must manage your emotions to reach a resolution.
- Consider the situation from the other person's perspective. Was there a reason that person didn't give you advance notice?
- Stand up for yourself. Address the issue with the person but do it objectively. Let them clearly know what you need them to do differently the next time.

CHAPTER 17
Manage Hardships and Turbulence

Over the course of your career, you will have many successes, build rich relationships, and enjoy your work. There will be times when you are recognized for your unique contribution to the organization and when you are appreciated by clients and coworkers. But one thing that is almost guaranteed is that you will also experience bad coworkers, office politics, untenable clients, and possibly being fired. How do I know this? Because I have seen it play out—not only personally, but with virtually everyone I have worked with at some point in their careers.

Does this sound fatalistic? Maybe so, but it is reality. I have already addressed the idea of being resilient, but I wanted to take a deeper dive into navigating turbulence. The good news is, because we all face turbulence at some point in our careers, we can prepare ahead of time to deal with it when it happens. I like to think that I have built a successful career over the course of the years. But I had my share of hardships along the way. I am going to share them with you because I learned important lessons from them all—even if it didn't feel like it at the time.

Ladder or Jungle Gym?

One of the most challenging situations in my career happened during a merger. I was offered a senior-level position in the new company—one level lower than I was before. At the time, I remembered Facebook Chief Operating Officer Sheryl Sandberg's comment that careers aren't really like ladders in which you just climb up or down. She said a career trajectory is ideally more like a jungle gym where you move up, down, and sideways along the way.[23] Sometimes it can be important to move laterally or even take a step back to advance.

What I did not anticipate was one of my former peer's reaction to the new order. I thought we had a stable, supportive relationship but he was soon to show his true colors. His new position was more senior, and he immediately tried to sabotage me and anyone who worked for me to grow his new department. In the previous chapter I used a personal example in which I did not initially handle a situation very well. In this example (and with the benefit of hindsight) I feel like I handled this situation the right way. Don't get me wrong. I was angry! Being blindsided like that was very emotional for me, but I tried to keep perspective. I had a choice to make. I could say, "This isn't working," and leave. Or I could reset and use the situation to implement a new business idea that I had in mind. With the help of my new boss and human resources business partner, we were able to create a new team to super-serve our most valuable clients.

At times I had to resist bringing the negativity and other emotions home with me at night. I stuck it out, focused on the work, and built my team. I told myself that I was going to take the high road in this situation by remaining professional and not taking on a victim mindset.

Eventually my colleague abruptly left the company. Fortunately I was able to build a strong bond with his successor. Sometimes your work life can change for the better overnight. Sometimes you do have to escape, and I considered it. But by sticking it out and doing my best work, I was able to build something that brought high value to the organization.

Joel's Take

When I think about how younger employees react when something bad happens to them at work, their reaction is predictable. They tend to react emotionally first. By the way, this isn't exclusive to young people, this is a common reaction for most human beings.

Let's say I got passed over for a promotion I thought I deserved. The way our brains work is that the emotions come first. I am already creating a story about how the process was unfair, how the person they selected is an idiot, how the hiring manager has it out for me, how nobody in this organization understands my contributions, and on and on. My feelings are hurt. I start to sulk, lash out, or demand an immediate explanation. I go back to my friends and coworkers and trash the people who made the decision. My brain has just handed my emotions the megaphone.

What is the best way to react when something bad happens at work? First, it's okay to have an emotional reaction. That is normal. What I am suggesting is to have that reaction in private and regroup. It is amazing what simply taking twenty-four hours to process the event can do for us. That doesn't mean that the next day finds us happy. It does mean that we have given our brains enough time to cycle through our initial emotional reaction and begin to get to a more analytical review of the situation. That is the point where you can follow up with your boss, reach out to the person who was promoted, and do whatever else you think you need to do to build back up in a professional way.

Thinking Ahead

If turbulence is predictable, then why are some people caught completely off guard when it happens to them? It might be because they aren't paying attention or ignoring warning signs. Other times it comes from their blindside and is brought about by something totally out of their control.

I can certainly relate to that. In June 2008, I was getting ready for a trip the next day to visit my team and clients in Los Angeles when an invitation from the president of Turner Ad Sales popped up on my calendar for 5 p.m. When I walked into David's office on the twenty-first floor of Time Warner Center and saw the vice president of human resources sitting there, my heart sank.

David told me that three senior executive roles were being eliminated, including my senior vice president position. He complimented me for my great work at Turner Broadcasting and told me the decision had nothing to do with performance. It was the recession of 2008, and measures were being taken to reduce several high-level executives and expenses. Fortunately, I was under contract, and the company was going to offer me additional severance. The biggest blow was that was my last day at Turner.

In a split second, I had no job and nowhere to go tomorrow. Obviously, my trip to Los Angeles was cancelled. The announcement was going to be made in the morning, and I couldn't go back to the office to say goodbye to my team. They would allow me to pack up my office in off hours.

Honestly, I don't remember how I made it back to my office on the nineteenth floor. I closed my door and tried to pull myself together. I called Joel and asked him to meet me at home ASAP. We had just moved into the city, around the corner from Time Warner Center, which, at that moment, seemed like a cruel irony.

Betsy on Fire

I immediately mobilized my network, especially some of my closest female colleagues that I knew from The WICT Network. This organization sponsors a female leadership program for women in the cable and telecommunications industry called The Betsy Magness Leadership Institute, in which I had participated. I made so many strong personal and professional connections there, and my first thought was to reach out to them. We have an expression we call "Betsy on fire" if anyone in the network needs help. So, I pulled the fire alarm!

One of my Betsy classmates gave me excellent advice on how to negotiate a better settlement package. Another counseled me to look for different opportunities that would build my skills and career repertoire. How right she turned out to be!

The key takeaway for me is that sometimes you must be pushed out of your comfort zone. Having my job at Turner eliminated was one of the best things that happened to me in my career. A year later I invited David to breakfast to thank him, and we continued to have a respectful, positive relationship.

Chapter Countdown

MAIN TAKEAWAYS FROM THIS CHAPTER:

- Hardships happen to everyone, and so does career turbulence.
- Careers are seldom a straight line. They are more of a zigzag based on advances and setbacks.
- Truly bad bosses, untrustworthy coworkers, and other reprehensible types eventually implode at some point— but it often takes a long time for it to happen.
- How you react to a setback is often more important to your career than the event itself.
- Sometimes you need to pull the alarm and lean on your network.

CHAPTER 18
Consider Corporate Culture

Organizations are like people in that they each have their own unique personality. If you look up the term "corporate culture," it commonly refers to the shared set of beliefs, practices, and values that can have a big impact on the way the people in that organization behave. It took me a while to understand the concept of corporate culture, but I can certainly say that about the different companies—from private to public, from small to large, from established to start-up—during my career.

Being aware of company culture can have a big impact on your work satisfaction and effectiveness. Learning about corporate culture goes beyond just reading the espoused value statements or photos of the work environment on the organization's webpage. It requires a deeper analysis and understanding of how people treat each other, what becomes a priority, and how decisions are made, among other things. The point is, you must pay attention to how people within an organization behave, not just what the company claims their culture to be.

Before You Say Yes
Sometimes, particularly early in your career, you are so glad to have a job offer that you jump at the chance to say yes. The corporate culture of the

hiring organization is not your prime concern. Plus, it can be tough to get a feel for an organization's culture based solely on the interview process. You are trying to make a good impression and so is the employer. Everyone is on their best behavior in the interview process, and you have a limited (if any) view into the culture. It's important to be thoughtful in your decision-making process and make sure that it's a good fit. It is not just about understanding that organization, but also understanding your own DNA and knowing what kind of environment you are looking for.

With the benefit of hindsight, I think back about the organizations I have worked with and can see that I have been exposed to a wide variety of corporate cultures. I started out in a small private company that was eventually sold to a larger company. Then I worked for very large corporations like Disney and Turner Broadcasting. After that I went to a start-up and worked there for over two years. That gig was an incredible experience for me but not the right fit for me. Over the course of my career, I have come to appreciate how much impact corporate culture can have on your fit and job satisfaction.

I also want to be realistic about what I mentioned at the start of the chapter. Sometimes you take a job so that you have a job. Any thoughts about culture are on a back burner, and you will make it work as you go. As I look back, I have kept track of some of the aspects of corporate culture that vary from one place to the next. The reality is it is not always black/white or either/or—most organizations are a blend.

This is not an exhaustive list but being aware of these aspects of an organization can help you consider the best fit for you.

- Large versus small
- Entrepreneurial versus entrenched

- Hierarchical versus flat
- Global versus domestic
- Start-up versus established
- Casual or formal?
- Work from home versus in-office
- Mission-driven versus profit-driven
- Promote from within or outside?
- Internal training?
- Support for working parents?
- For start-ups, is there a human resources department?
- Organization-sponsored social activities or do your own thing?

Culture Within the Culture

Within organizations, different divisions, office locations, and even work groups can have their own cultures. At Spectrum Reach, our advertising sales division works hard to build on our corporate culture by defining and prioritizing values and beliefs within our group. Employees who are nurtured and grow help us to be the best that we can be for our clients. That, in turn, helps us deliver on our goals to the corporation.

There are creative ways to find out about the culture of an organization. If it is a public company, check out their "investors" page of their website. You can usually find a copy of their annual report and additional information that can help you understand more about their culture. Even though the annual report is a place where most organizations want to put their best foot forward, you can get a perspective that might be deeper than their general "about" page. It often gives you a good sense as to what the company stands for and what their pro-social goals are. If it is a small organization, do a search about the company in the local newspaper's website. There will likely be better coverage of their activities than you would find in national sources.

In our world of rater reviews, you can also check out sources like Glassdoor, although I always urge people to be careful to place too much weight on Glassdoor reviews. There are people who say the only people who take the time to write Glassdoor reviews are ex-employees with an axe to grind. Use it carefully as only one data point in your research.

The Culture in Your Current Organization

Paying attention to culture is not just something you do when sizing up a potential employer. It is also a factor that you should be aware of in whatever job you already have. I have always tried to be savvy about the culture of the organizations I worked in while also being true to myself. Some elements of an organization's culture are visible. Are people still coming to an office and wearing formal business attire? In which case, if you show up in jeans and sneakers, would you be considered unprofessional? Or do you work for a company that's more casual, and if you show up in a suit you look out of place?

Much of an organization's culture is harder to see and is mostly associated with the way people behave. For example, nowadays many companies have a policy that permits people to work from home—at least for part of the week. That's great, but what do people do? Are the people considered on an upward track working from home every day? Or are they in the office most days?

From my experience, one of the most important aspects of how a company's culture operates is seeing how decisions get made. Much of this is done behind the scenes and requires paying attention, listening, and asking questions to understand it better.

Joel's Take

I've worked for several different companies over the years, and the culture in each was distinctly different. Sometimes the difference was jarring, and I had to adapt quickly. One example was when I worked at Cahners Publishing. It was a highly structured and formal corporate culture. There were clear and well-developed assignments and responsibilities. There was also a lot of traditional employee support structures in place to help you get your work done. If I had any need for supplies, IT help, HR questions, or anything else, there was a person and phone number to call to get what I needed.

As a result, it was a bit of culture shock when I left Cahners and took a job at Marvel. At the time, Marvel was morphing from a comic book publishing company to a giant entertainment company. This was a huge change, and there was tremendous flux. We were literally trying to get our act together to have comic book people introduce promotion and licensing and move the company to the digital, film, and television world. But the comic book culture was still firmly in place when I got there. Everything was very loosey-goosey and there was no formal support in place. I was issued a broken chair and a wobbly table to use as a desk. There were no scheduled meetings and no formalized structure of any type that I remember.

That really threw me for a loop because I wasn't used to just sitting in my office and not collaborating or having formalized meetings with coworkers to move things forward. I didn't do a very good job of anticipating what working in such an unstructured environment would be like. I wonder now if I had known what that first year was going to be like, would I have still taken the job? In hindsight I'm glad I did because Marvel turned into a powerhouse in the entertainment media world and eventually, I was able to figure out how to work in that culture and collaborate to contribute to Marvel's

success during that transition. But because I didn't do my homework before I joined, it was a shock, and it took me months to adapt—even though I consider myself pretty flexible and adaptable.

Whether you are interviewing for a job, new in a role, aspiring to advance, or hoping to make the best contribution you can to your organization, understanding corporate culture can go a long way toward helping you be successful and more engaged in your work.

Chapter Countdown

MAIN TAKEAWAYS FROM THIS CHAPTER:

- Understanding the culture of an organization is critical to your long-term happiness.
- Culture is what is behaved and rewarded, not what the organization puts on their coffee mugs or website.
- When considering working for an organization, do the research ahead of time to understand their work culture.
- You don't have to completely conform to a company's culture, but you will never be happy if you are fighting against it.
- If you go from one culture to another, like any change, give yourself time to adjust.

CHAPTER 19
Prepare for Leadership Opportunities

You are building your career rocket as you fly it. You will be making decisions as you go that will influence your career trajectory. After some period of successfully doing whatever you were hired to do, it is highly likely that you will be approached to manage other people. This might happen sooner than you think.

This chapter is not about "how to be a manager." There are scores of books and articles on the subject. It is about helping you think ahead about your own career path and the opportunities ahead.

What If I Don't Want to Be a Manager?
Let's address this first. You might not think you want to be a manger. That's okay—it's definitely not for everyone, and you might be surprised at how many people share this preference.

If this sounds like you, it is important to take an open and honest look at your reason for saying no. Ask yourself, "Why not?" Does it not fit your temperament? What are you afraid of? Do you really know what's involved? Did you have a bad boss in the past who left a bad taste for the job? Will it take you away from doing the hands-on work you enjoy and find rewarding? Did you somehow develop a "we versus they" attitude about management that you need to reconsider?

If you are offered a management-related job and you decline, you need to have a reason that holds up to the facts of your situation. Saying no to a management role in some organizations can be interpreted (or misinterpreted) as a lack of ambition. It can also be seen as a lack of commitment to the organization and its mission. In some organizations you might not get a second chance if you say no the first time around.

There is another potential downside to passing on a managerial role. Some organizations do not have a non-management advancement track. That could mean a ceiling on earnings and other advancement opportunities for individual contributors.

Are There Other Options?

Some organizations do offer alternative career paths that provide advancement opportunities for individual contributors and specialists based on expertise. If you think that is your preference, it's something you want to ask about when you join a company. If it is your goal, how do you strive to be the best person there is at that specialty? This often involves building your reputation outside your company—publishing, speaking at conferences, blogging, podcasting, or becoming an influencer on the subject.

Often start-ups and nontraditional organizations provide more opportunity for this track. They can be flatter and more flexible. More traditional organizations tend to be more layered.

Team Leader as a Hybrid

You might consider becoming the lead for a project team. This offers a hybrid role that lands between individual contributor and traditional manager. This role still requires your technical or specialized expertise, but also positions you to manage others in their roles on the team. You would lead team members toward the project outcome and mentor new people, but you might not have to deal with the managerial details for those people.

You might discover that you like it and are good at it. So much of effective management is treating people the way you want to be treated. I would encourage readers of this book to try it, especially since it is easier to test this out early in your career.

What If I Do Want to Be a Manager?

One of the recurring themes in this book is that so much of rocketing our potential involves open reflection and honest self-awareness. What strengths and experiences do you bring to this opportunity? Where do you think you fall short? Is there a way to connect with a mentor to address those areas? Can you "toe-dip" by holding up your hand to volunteer for assignments in which there is a leadership role? I can tell you that from an executive perspective, when someone volunteers to lead a project, even if it is not directly related to the business, I am grateful. For example, I have seen people gain valuable experience and really shine spearheading the company holiday Toys for Tots effort and other voluntary and informal roles. Getting involved in one of your company's business resource groups for which you have a personal passion (e.g., women's group, LGBTQ, multicultural) can be a great opportunity to build project management and leadership skills. Plus, the role may provide exposure for those individuals to upper management that would take years to build in their everyday roles.

If you think you want to pursue a management/leadership track, go for it. Act. Don't sit back and wait. Have an open discussion with your manager about your career trajectory. Ask them if they think you are ready. If not, what do they think you need to do to be considered? What would they need to see from you over the course of the year for them to consider you ready? Is there a way the organization can support this goal?

Manage the Potential Downsides Before They Become a Problem

Becoming a leader can change the work dynamic, especially if you move up within your own work group. People who were once peers are possibly your direct reports. You might fall out of that social group, or at least you will be considered differently by the members. You will be under more scrutiny than as an individual employee. You may have to be more hands-off than you naturally want to be. It would be expected that you delegate more. Can you do that?

I will admit my bias and say that I believe one of the most rewarding aspects of work is leading a successful group, team, department, or business. At the same time, you have incredible opportunity to have a positive impact on the lives of others. If that is part of your higher purpose, I encourage you to go all out!

Chapter Countdown

MAIN TAKEAWAYS FROM THIS CHAPTER:

- Do you really want to be a manager? It's not for everyone.
- If not, be clear on why not so that you can explain it in a way that doesn't suggest a lack of ambition.
- The path to advancement in most organizations typically involves increased people management responsibility. If that's not for you, look for organizations with dual-path advancement opportunities.
- If you do want to take on management responsibilities, discuss it with your boss. Ask for feedback.
- More responsibility can come with more headaches, but the personal and professional rewards can be the best part of a working life.

CHAPTER 20
Stretch Yourself to Stay Relevant

———

Since the name of this book is *Rocket Your Potential* and you have read this far, you are probably someone with ambition and are not the kind of person who wants to remain standing in one place. If you are happy to stay at the level you are and do the work you are currently doing, this chapter is probably not for you. On the other hand, if you are ready to think seriously about what you need to do to move on and move up, keep reading.

Anticipate Change

In today's rapidly evolving business world, no matter what industry or discipline you're involved with, nothing is staying the same. The only thing that's constant is change. The world of technology and processes is changing and evolving so rapidly that even if you have a strong skill set, you need to continue to nurture and grow that skill set by adding additional skills to your toolkit.

This chapter builds upon everything that we've been talking about in previous parts of the book—from passionate curiosity to doing your homework. But, wherever you are in your career, you need to keep stretching and commit to being a lifelong learner. Your best bet is to raise your awareness to identify what you need to know today and what you may need to know for tomorrow.

I have seen it play out repeatedly at the companies for which I have worked. The young people who were willing to stretch themselves by learning new soft and hard skills were perceived as more competent and advanced faster. They also developed increased self-esteem by being able to tackle work that was beyond their daily function.

Skills are one thing to build on, but I'm also talking about increasing your breadth of experience, which increases your value to your organization. For example, we have all heard the expression "working in silos." One way to go beyond a silo existence is to experience different aspects of a business. Understanding the different functions and perspectives of the different work groups in your organization helps you to be more well-rounded and to have a breadth and depth of experience and expertise. I have always tried to continue to build expertise and add breadth to make me more valuable and more marketable, but to also keep me challenged and interested.

Be Ready to Stretch Yourself

At some point in your career, you will have an opportunity to take on an assignment, a new role, or a new job without having specific expertise in that area. You must be ready to make that leap of faith to rocket your career. Then you stretch—you will have to quickly learn as you go, and it might seem like you are building the plane while you're flying it.

Joel's Take

I started my career in sales with one of the world's largest pharmaceutical companies. It was a huge organization, and at one point produced five of the top ten selling drugs in America. I did well there as a salesperson. I made a nice living and was known as a high performer. But I took the long-range view to my career early on. I realized that I didn't want to just be a salesperson forever.

Expanding my horizons and having an expanded knowledge of business was my goal, understanding how brands grow and how marketing was that tool. I knew my company wasn't going to send me to school to make that happen, so I became friendly with the brand managers and other marketing disciplines. I would always visit them when I traveled to our headquarters and take them out to lunch or for a cup of coffee. I learned so much just from being around them and hearing about the problems they were facing and, as a result, it helped me understand their world. They were very generous with their opinions and patient with my questions. I asked them what their pie chart was all about, what they did day-to-day, what hard and soft skills they recommended for me. I was curious about how they determined what kind of material to create to send to consumers. From those conversations, in addition to studying books on marketing, I expanded my knowledge, my breadth, and my business acumen.

I decided to stretch myself to be relevant in the future. I had to take the lead on my own future. After all, I was a speech and theatre major in college! I knew that if I was going to stay relevant in business, I would have to take the initiative to create my own path. I didn't even know what the word marketing meant but I was willing to work hard and I had the desire to grow. That served me well as I continued to grow in the company, reach higher-level jobs, earn more income, and eventually that job was my springboard into the publishing industry. I wasn't just a salesperson anymore. I was somebody who, because of my own initiatives, early in my career, became more valuable to any kind of organization. I would have never reached the salary, responsibility, or satisfaction level in my career if I had just remained that pharmaceutical salesman trying to convince a doctor to use our pills.

I still think about having lunch with and reaching out to those marketing people early in my career. I have worked hard at maintaining the courage and the willingness to reach out to people to learn the things that can stretch me. I would not have been as successful in the business world with my career had I not done that.

You Are Your Rocket Pilot

Rocketing your potential is about taking control of your own destiny. You can't expect anybody to hand you all the answers or all the solutions. You must have the passion, the curiosity, and the courage. You also must be willing to come out of your shell, and it's never easy to leave our comfort zones. This philosophy applies whether it's your first job or your twentieth job. We talked in Chapter 5 about the importance of finding a mentor. One of the most important links to getting from where you are to where you want to be is finding people who can advise you. Seek out people who are willing to spend some time giving you honest opinions and useful guidance.

Sometimes knowing how to start is the hardest part. We have created a simple worksheet below that you can complete to help get you started thinking in these terms. You will see that the worksheet contains four columns.

Column 1: What you are good at and like doing?

In the first column place everything that you believe you're good at and you enjoy doing. What are the parts of your job that give you energy?

Column 2: What you are not good at and think you will need?

In the second column you should capture what is it that you're not adept at doing, and what needs to be added to your portfolio to progress in your career. For example, maybe you are not naturally analytical and don't know your way around spreadsheets. Perhaps you are not good at public speaking and it's hurting your career advancement.

Column 3: Create a roadmap to get you there.
The third column becomes a roadmap to take you where you want to be. Perhaps you can take an online course to learn basic accounting and spreadsheet use. Maybe you can sign up for Toastmasters class to help you become more comfortable with public speaking.

Column 4: Who can help you?
In the fourth column, capture the names of the people within or outside of your network who can advise, teach, serve as role models, or otherwise support you.

What you are good at and like doing?	What you will need in the future.	How you will get there.	Who can help you?

The Importance of Other People in Your Career Trajectory

While all four columns are an important part of this quick self-assessment, in my opinion, the most critical is the fourth column. You can't do this alone. If you are early in your career, currently in your first or second job out of school, and you want to grow your career and get promoted, you need to ask your manager or your boss if there are any skills that you need to acquire for them to consider you for advancement. It is the best way to get a quick understanding of what they think you are missing right now. You must put in the work. Some organizations have formal development pathways for junior staff, but in other organizations you might have to structure it yourself. Speak to the supervisors and tell them that you want to learn more and see if you can shadow them for a day. Ask if there is an assignment they could give you to expose you to other parts of the business. Be creative and look for ways to be helpful while stretching yourself.

Myth: People Will Recognize Your Genius

It is not uncommon to find people early in their careers who think that they will be recognized and promoted by virtue of how smart they are. Let's consider the following example. Maria is a bright engineer in her second year with her company. She graduated near the top of her class from a prestigious engineering school and had several attractive job offers. Once hired, she focused on her work and took pride in being accurate, efficient, and being right. She started noticing that others she worked with were getting promoted or put on interesting project teams while she stayed in place.

In frustration she confronted her boss about why she was getting passed over. Her manager was honest with her and told her that she needed to improve her interpersonal skills with coworkers. The other people being promoted may not have shown Maria's technical expertise but were easier to work with and did a better job of relating to people. The manager had discussed this with her on previous occasions, but it took getting passed over for Maria to pay attention. Her boss gently but clearly said that it isn't enough to be smart. She said that the company is full of smart people. You must be smart *and* be someone who can work well with others. Maria's challenge was to stretch herself to stay relevant and be effective in the long run.

In summary, we all have areas that we are good at and enjoy doing. As human beings, we all have areas where we could do better. The key is to identify those areas for yourself, get help from others in developing the areas you target, and put in the work to rocket your potential.

Chapter Countdown
MAIN TAKEAWAYS FROM THIS CHAPTER:

- Be aware of the skills needed to be successful in the future—not just today.
- Challenge yourself to stretch and go outside your comfort zone.
- Be honest with yourself about what you want from work and where you want to go. Then, create a plan.
- Smart is good, but sometimes it only gets you in the door.
- Tap into your network to help you in flight

Section

4

SOAR TO NEW HEIGHTS

CHAPTER 21
Ace Your Internal Interview

One of the best places to grow your career may be at your current company. If you want to change jobs, move up, or make a lateral move, you should start by exploring potential internal opportunities. In fact, LinkedIn's Global Talent Trends 2020 report found 73% of human resources and hiring professionals said that internal recruiting is increasingly important to their company.[24] And employees also stay longer—41% longer—at companies that focus on retaining talent and recruiting from within. At Spectrum Reach, we encourage movement across our markets and departments and try to prioritize and promote internal candidates. That being said, it's incumbent upon employees to impress.

Interview Like an External Candidate

While recently staffing my new Client Success team, some of the internal candidates we interviewed excelled while others bombed. Why? Preparation and approaching the process like an external candidate was the difference. For example, one candidate for a senior manager position highlighted her accomplishments in previous roles at the company in a short PowerPoint presentation. She talked about her management style and included some fun facts about herself. Even though I already knew her, she interviewed for the job as if we were meeting for the first time. In sharp contrast, another candidate for a director position interviewed poorly. He did not take the time to do his homework on the role or my background and previous roles at the company, which would have been an opportunity to demonstrate his preparation. He did not come to the interview with a thoughtful presentation. You can guess who got the job and who didn't.

Internal candidates have an inside track on the company's products, people, and processes. It's critical to demonstrate your "insider" knowledge and ability to get up to speed quickly in an expanded or new role. Develop and be prepared to discuss a high-level 30-60-90-day plan to showcase your strategic vision for the position as well as tactics for flawless execution.

Joel's Take

When I was an executive at Warner Bros., there was an important role I needed to fill. The ideal candidate would be charged with working with major clients to create exciting cross promotions with DC Comics superheroes, including Batman and Superman. Pretty cool, huh? My recruiting team presented numerous external candidates with soft and hard skills and experience that matched my needs. One internal candidate also reached out. She had good experience in another department but didn't quite have the exact background and skills for this position. I interviewed her out of courtesy, and she wowed the heck out of me! Why? Because she did her homework. She had interviewed other members of my team, asked for examples of the actual work on our plates, learned more about my style (as she would be my direct report), and even spoke to one or two of our clients. Impressive. She was prepared and ready for the challenge of convincing me—big time. She even knew how much I loved happy, outgoing, and smiling energy with all of my staff. Cindy got the job and became an integral member of our department. When I left Warner Bros. several years later to run my own educational marketing company, one of the first things I did was hire Cindy. To this day, I would hire Cindy for anything and everything.

Tell a Story

Make a list of potential questions you may be asked and craft your best answers ahead of time. Nothing beats practicing your answers out loud to make sure it flows. Practice in front of your cat. Better yet, build your muscle memory by asking a friend, family member, or colleague to role play with you. Bring your experience and skills to life with brief, relevant stories and examples.

Describe how you tackled a real business situation, using the STAR behavioral interview format popularized by leadership consulting firm DDI (situation, task, action, and result). Illustrate how you provided value to a company priority or how you overcame a challenge. These candid stories can highlight your decision-making capabilities and quantifiable achievements. For example, since one of my strong skills is creating and building new teams, I might tell the following story:

I was originally hired at Time Warner Cable Media to oversee and transform a regional marketing team of twenty-five people. The first thing I did was learn the business needs and challenges by speaking to and visiting sales leaders in the respective markets. Then I assessed the talent by meeting with each team member individually, reviewing performance reviews, and consulting with my new colleagues. I developed an initial plan, gained consensus from my human resources business partners, and then presented the plan to my new boss. The plan included 30-60-90-day action steps, with a check-in with my boss every thirty days to assess progress and results. The result was a significant team transformation that helped drive revenue results and marketing and sales team collaboration.

Be Likeable

According to one of my trusted human resources business partners, the single most important thing hiring managers say after an interview is "I *liked* her or him." Think about that. We put hours into preparing our resume, our LinkedIn profile, and other social presence. Yet we cannot overlook the importance of this emotional gateway. It makes sense because in an ideal workplace, we want to like the people we work with. So, even before discussing your skill sets, look for a way to connect with your next potential boss. For example, if you're naturally more of an introvert, think about how you can come out of your shell to make that important first impression. LinkedIn profiles can provide you with helpful nuggets of information, including former jobs, hobbies, or involvement in alumni, industry, or pro-social organizations. These nuggets can be great conversation-starters or icebreakers. Be genuine and bring a positive spark to the conversation.

At the end of an internal interview, ask, "What else do you need to convince you I am the right person for the role?" or "What does great look like in this role?" When I interview job candidates, my last question is an open-ended, "What other questions do you have?" Their response is telling. Well-prepared and curious candidates may ask something about my career experience, commitment to female leadership, or an additional question about the company or team. Always try to take advantage of an opportunity to find out another key nugget of information. Finally, within twenty-four hours, send a compelling thank you email or hand-written note. Reiterate your passion for the position and commitment to making an increased contribution to the team and company.

Chapter Countdown

MAIN TAKEAWAYS FROM THIS CHAPTER:

- Prepare and interview for internal jobs as if you were an external candidate.
- Create a 30-60-90-day plan for yourself in the role and be able to describe it during an interview.
- Write down the questions you anticipate getting in the interview, then practice answering them out loud.
- Use brief, relevant stories as examples.
- Be prepared with questions to ask the interviewer.

CHAPTER 22
Know When It Is Time to Move On

Most of us are so focused on getting a job that we put very little thought into ever leaving a job until forced by circumstances. The truth is, that process should require as much thought and clarity as finding a job. So, what do you do when that little voice in the back of your mind gets increasingly louder and is now shouting at you that it's time to leave your job?

You're Not Alone

The days of getting a job right out of college and then retiring from the same company fifty years later are long over. Over time I have seen job tenure getting shorter, and the research backs that up. Career expert Amy Gallo reports that 70% of people quit their first job within two years.[25] The younger you are, the shorter the stay. The current trend, even beyond your first couple of jobs, is toward shorter tenure. The Bureau of Labor Statistics reports that employees aged 25-34 remain in their jobs for an average of only 2.8 years. By comparison, tenure for 55–64-year-olds is almost 10 years.[26] How long you stay in your job is also partly a function of the industry you work in. For example, faster turnover in the technology sector and at start-ups is more common than in traditional fields like banking and finance. The reality is that almost everyone quits jobs and moves on. It is a natural part of our economy and a normal part of building a career. Knowing when it is time for you to take the leap will help reduce your stress when the time comes.

When I review a resume, I expect to see job transitions, especially early in one's career. That's a normal part of developing your career over time. There are many legitimate reasons for leaving a job after a short stay. Sometimes people are concerned that they will appear as "job-hoppers" if they have moved around a lot. That can be a concern if the person is twenty years into their work career and has changed jobs every year or two. But for someone at the front stage of their career, I consider it a part of normal job progress history, especially if the candidate shows the movement was to support their personal or professional trajectory.

Pay Attention to the Warning Signs

Unfortunately, there is no one-size-fits-all list to know when to leave a job. Everyone is different, and there are hundreds of combinations of personalities, people, and expectations. No job is perfect, and anyone will tell you work is made up of good days and bad days. However, it might be time for you to leave if you consistently feel like you are:

- Bored
- Not challenged
- Not excited about the work
- Dreading going in to work most days
- Not growing or learning
- Being expected to act in an unethical manner
- Unable to see a path forward for yourself
- Not aligned with the values or mission of the organization
- Working for an organization that is in financial trouble.

Much of what I am describing is about fit. Several women I know have taken jobs with start-ups. For some of them, the excitement and risk fed their energy. For others, they were attracted to what sounded like a cool and hip work environment, which didn't turn out to be right for them. One woman that I mentored discovered that she could not adjust to the reality of the start-up culture. That became clear to her after a few weeks when she discovered the environment was very different from what the person who hired her described. The founder was twenty-seven years old and told her, "I really don't like working with people." There was no human resources department, few processes in place, and the working environment felt to her like the Wild, Wild West. Personnel issues were either ignored or handled in an unprofessional manner.

As mentioned previously in this book, one of my career stops was at the prestigious Walt Disney Company. They hired me to be the editor in chief of *Disney Adventures*, their magazine for kids aged seven to fourteen. I thought it would be my dream job at my dream company. After being there for just a few months, I quickly started seeing some troubling warning signs. The business model was flawed and the magazine was operating in the red. There was tremendous corporate pressure and politics to deliver revenues and profits. As a result of the financial pressures, there was a revolving door of bosses—four in two years. And for some reason, the last boss I had there just didn't like me. This was difficult for me because I had always had good bosses in the past and always had good working relationships with all of them. Other red flags added to the evidence that the job and company might not be the right place for me. I was being left out of key meetings and wasn't asked to work on any of the additional projects that were going on in our group. It became clear to me that the decision about my long-term career potential in this role at Disney had already been determined.

Ultimately, I made the decision to explore other opportunities and leave Disney. To the outside world, my position at one of the world's top entertainment companies seemed as magical as the Magic Kingdom. But I could read all the signs and knew my career wasn't going anywhere if I stayed in that job. Disappointed and dejected, my short-term strategy was to keep my head down and continue to do the best job I could in that job. I continually tried to build a bond with my current boss and other team members. I tried to take emotion out of it. Earlier in my career, a previous boss gave me great advice. She said, "Don't be a victim. If you feel things aren't working out for you, take control of your own destiny. Make your own plan. It might take time to do that, but that's okay." Another excellent piece of advice I received—and now give others—is, when possible, don't run away from a job. Instead, run to a new opportunity.

The first thing I did was to reach out to my personal and professional network. I cannot overstate the importance of building and nourishing your network (which is why we dedicate an entire chapter to the importance of network development). Through this network I was able to make a pivot from editorial to sales and marketing by landing a job at Turner Broadcasting. It turned out to be the best thing that could have happened, taking my career on a completely new trajectory at a time when kids' cable television soared while kids' magazines struggled. Sadly, *Disney Adventures* eventually folded.

Should You Quit Before You Land Another Job?

In an ideal world, you would have the next job in hand before you quit your current job. The reality is, sometimes you must leave a job right away and you don't have the next job lined up. There might be circumstances that require that you leave immediately. Maybe it is a toxic workplace. Perhaps you are being harassed or feel unsafe for some reason. Possibly you discovered that the organization is conducting activities that are questionable or even illegal.

Those can all be situations where your priority should be to remove yourself from the situation first and then start a new job search.

There can be downsides for quitting without another job. The obvious one is the lack of income and benefits. Also, whether it is fair or not, prospective employers tend to consider a candidate more favorably if they are holding a job than if they are not. For the most part, unless it is a large gap between jobs, it will not be a deal-breaker, but you should be prepared to discuss the gap. Remember to respond in an honest, professional, and positive way.

Should You Stick with It?

What if you have only been in your job for a couple months? Should you stick it out longer?

That depends. If you have already made up your mind to leave, there is a convincing case for just tearing off the Band-Aid and giving your notice right away. One of my colleagues tells a story that is probably more common than we think. When she graduated from college and started interviewing, she accepted the first job she was offered. It wasn't her dream entry-level job, but she didn't have any other interviews lined up, and it seemed like all her friends already found jobs. So, she took the job—and knew within a few weeks that she had made a big mistake. The company culture was hyper-competitive and collaboration was almost non-existent. She was thrown in to sink or swim, and she received little support from her manager. She was so stressed it started affecting her sleep, eating habits, and her mood. She quit after two months. As difficult as that was for her, she talks about everything she learned from that hardship and how it helped her make future job decisions. She also said it has made her a much better manager.

From my perspective as a manager, I would rather have someone tell me that they are quitting after the first week rather than tell me several months into it. Because we invest in their onboarding heavily on the front end, we will be committing many resources including the time and energy of their coworkers to get them up to speed. That commitment takes them away from other work, and it is not something we can recover when you quit after five months. An article in *Forbes* is clear on this subject, "The cost of a departing employee rises every day that they delay the decision if it is indeed inevitable."[27] You might feel guilty about quitting so soon but consider the impact from your employer's point of view.

Zappos, known for its mission to "deliver WOW through service," has a program that pays new employees up to $4,000 to quit the company after initial training sessions. The policy was designed to ensure that new hires are the right fit for the company culture and are committed to working beyond just a paycheck.

Remove Emotion

Making the decision to quit is not easy. As humans we need to acknowledge and cycle through the emotions we are feeling before we can get to that part of our thinking that is rational and fact-based. Depending on your circumstances, you might be angry, worried, embarrassed, or even feel like you have failed. Those are all understandable, and it is normal to feel what you are feeling. As you create your exit plan, you will be able to make a clearer, more objective plan if you take time to first work through the emotional reactions you are having. Try making a list of everything you feel. Think about both the best and worst possible scenarios and outcomes of making a change. If you're comfortable, discuss your feelings and potential plan with family, friends, or close business confidantes. Talking it out may help ground you and give you a different perspective on the situation or ways to approach a change.

Have You Tried Everything?

Before you pull the plug, have you exhausted other viable alternatives to quitting? Have you talked with your boss about other options such as taking on other responsibilities or working at your organization in a different role? It's possible that there might be ways your boss could work with you to address your concerns. Are there other projects that you could get involved with that are beyond your daily tasks? Can you raise your hand to volunteer for other organizational initiatives? Doing so would expose you to other parts of your organization, other people, and perhaps other job opportunities.

How to Quit

Whatever your reason for leaving your job, above everything else, handle your departure in a responsible, professional, and respectful matter.

- Tell your boss first—before you tell your coworkers, before you tell your friends, and before you tell HR. Your boss should never hear it from someone else.

- If possible, tell your boss in person—this isn't the place to email, text, or even call if you are in the same location.

- Prepare. I suggest that you go so far as to write out a short script. Practice it. You wouldn't read it to your boss, of course, but the act of writing it out will give you confidence help you stay on topic when the time comes.

- Stay positive. Of course, your boss will want to know why you are leaving. Don't criticize the organization or any of the people you work with. Talk about it from your perspective, about how the role was not a fit for you, was different than you thought it would be, does not fit into your career plan, or whatever your circumstances are.

....

- Be prepared for questions. Don't be surprised if your boss asks something like, "What will it take for you to stay?" Think this through ahead of time. Are there some things that, if changed, would entice you to stay? If not, thank her or him for asking, and stay firm.

....

- Your boss might be caught off guard, so keep the meeting short. He or she will need time to adjust to your news and their next steps. Don't try to solve other problems in this meeting.

....

- Remember that bosses have a career and most likely have quit jobs before, too. They can probably understand what it feels like to be in your current shoes—even if they don't admit it.

....

- Be gracious and be genuine. Thank your boss for the opportunities you have had, even if the job hasn't worked out for you.

....

- Give at least two weeks' notice. Unless your organization has other guidelines, that is a minimum expectation. Your organization might try to negotiate a longer departure window so that you can help transition someone else into the role. Or they might tell you that they would like you to leave immediately, especially if you are going to a competitor. Be prepared for either scenario by having a response in mind.

....

- Beware the exit interview. These are typically conducted by someone in human resources and possibly with your manager as well. Continue to be professional and positive. They will probably ask you for feedback about your experience with the organization. Do not see this as an opportunity to "tell them what you think of them, once and for all." Do not speak for others, and do not use this as a therapy session. Be honest but professional and gracious. It does not pay to burn bridges.

Remember that everyone must leave a job at some point in their career, and most of us do it multiple times. Be clear on your reasons, be firm in your decisions, and be professional—and then take the next step for what is best for you and your career.

Chapter Countdown
MAIN TAKEAWAYS FROM THIS CHAPTER:

- Understand that it is normal to change jobs, particularly early in your career.
- Know the warning signs that tell you it is time for a change.
- Try to take emotions out of your decision if you can.
- Consider the alternatives before quitting.
- Leave a job professionally, and don't burn any bridges.

CHAPTER 23
Pay it Forward

___

This chapter is a change of pace. Up until now we have discussed getting what you need to rocket your potential, including self-awareness, networks, resilience, and many other tactical skills and perspectives. This chapter focuses on something more strategic. This chapter is about what you can give others, and it gives me a chance to talk to you about something that I believe is a true superpower. I'm talking about paying it forward. What does that mean, exactly?

What It Means to Pay It Forward

First, let's start with an expression we all understand, "Pay it back." When someone does something thoughtful, considerate, kind, or beneficial to you in any way, you return the favor to them. Here's a simple example: "You paid for lunch last time; today is my turn." By comparison, when paying it *forward*, you return a kindness, but to someone else. Let's say you had a more experienced coworker who made it a point to make you feel welcome at work for the first couple weeks you were there. You would pay that forward by extending that kindness to a new hire in your company. Maybe you decide to pay that kindness forward not just once (which is more common when paying someone *back*). Rather, you decide you are always going to pay that forward to *every* new hire in your office.

Now imagine if each of those people you pay it forward to decides, based the kindness you showed them, to pay it forward to multiple other people. Pretty soon, the power of paying it forward becomes a multiplier and can create a massive positive ripple effect.

One of the great things about paying it forward is that you can start right now. It doesn't require reading up, watching online instructional videos, or going to some training program. You just do it by doing it. It doesn't require seniority or—best of all—permission. You could be any age and any level in an organization and still find ways to pay thoughtfulness forward. Some of them will be small gestures, others more sweeping, but they will all be appreciated.

Joel's Take

Phyllis has done a great job of assembling tips and suggestions for you to rocket your potential based on her experience over the course of her impressive career. Some of them you can use right away, and others will come in handy down the road.

One of the important things you can do right now is understanding what she is describing here about paying it forward and how you might put it into action for yourself. It is one of the ways in which we can change other people's lives. I don't mean to overstate it, but I believe in it that strongly. I have strived to pay forward for my whole life, so I guess it comes easy for me. That is not a brag . . . it just is. I sometimes wonder how this became such an important part of who I am. I still haven't figured that out, but it has caused me to try to share the importance of paying it forward to others.

Paying it forward is a way to make your own life richer right away by helping others. There is a lot to be said for simple random acts of kindness but to me, paying it forward is going a bit deeper. It involves a degree of introspection and reflection about what others did for you that you found helpful. Then comes the most satisfying part—how and with whom can you pay it forward? To me there is nothing more rewarding than advancing a kindness or assistance to someone who is not expecting it and can benefit from your thoughtfulness.

Look for Opportunities

Paying it forward is a mindset. You will know that you have established a pay-it-forward mindset when you find yourself looking for ways to make it happen, both at work and in your personal life. It is a great way to create a richer life for others and for yourself. The biggest motivation for me to write this book is to pay forward all the kindnesses and consideration people have done for me across my career and personal life. The way people have done that for me is a very long list. Many of the stories I tell in the book are examples of things people did for me that I continue to try to pay forward. While it is not an exhaustive list, here are some kindnesses people have done for me that I have strived to pay forward. By the way, some of these were "tough love" and didn't feel so kind in the moment. But with the benefit of hindsight, I know the person had my best interest at heart and I am eternally grateful for the honesty.

- Involving me on projects outside of my daily job duties
- Giving me direct feedback when I needed to hear it
- Pushing me out of my comfort zone to try something new
- Connecting me with someone in their network who they thought could be helpful to me
- Spending time helping me learn a new skill
- Helping one of our kids get a summer internship
- Inviting my family to a special VIP event

- Singing my praises and/or giving me exposure to senior executives
- Coaching me on public speaking
- Setting me straight when I wasn't seeing things clearly

Paying it forward enriches your own life. Not only will it provide you with the satisfaction of helping others, but there are also health benefits to you for paying it back. Research has established links to paying it back and forward, including lower blood pressure, higher self-esteem, less depression, and even a longer lifespan.[28] Wow!

I encourage young people to not think about career advancement myopically. It's easy to think about getting a promotion in terms of more money. Let's face it, who doesn't like having more money? Money can make life easier—up to a point. But instead of thinking about your promotion being the avenue to a new car or better furniture, think about it as a new platform to do more to enrich the lives of others while creating physical and emotional benefits for yourself.

Capture It in Writing

For those of you who find it easier to have some structure to get started, here's my worksheet to provide a framework for thinking about paying it forward. It starts by asking you to reflect on the ways people helped you in your life and career. The second step is to identify the person or people to whom you want to pay it forward. The last step is to decide how you will, specifically, pay it forward. This framework is simply intended to get you thinking in these terms. The most important part is to just get started.

What are the ways other people helped you in your career or personal life?	Who could benefit from you paying it forward to them?	How and when can you pay it forward to them?

Social scientists have done research showing that the effect of a single act of kindness can have a ripple effect that sets off subsequent chains of generosity that reach far beyond the original act.[29] Paying it forward is a powerful way to have a direct impact on others beyond your personal reach. It can also increase your own satisfaction with the way you contribute to the world. What are you waiting for?

Chapter Countdown

MAIN TAKEAWAYS FROM THIS CHAPTER:

- Paying it forward can have a multiplier effect that goes far beyond your initial effort.
- Others benefit when you pay it forward, but so do you.
- Start small, and go from there.
- Advancing your own career gives you more leverage to pay it forward to others.
- Start today!

CHAPTER 24
Rocket Your Higher Purpose

If you are reading this book, you are probably getting started in your professional life and feel like you must figure everything out as you go. Maybe you are in your first or second job out of college and starting to build some momentum, but you probably feel like there are so many unknown variables ahead of you that it makes it hard to plan anything long-term.

Looking Way Down the Road

It reminds me of when I finished college and started working. On my first day at work the human resources person sat me down and asked me how much of my paycheck I wanted to go into my retirement account. Retirement? I was twenty-one years old and had my whole life ahead of me. The last thing on my mind was retirement! Little did I know how important those contributions (and the power of compounding) would benefit me later in my life. It just seemed, at the time, odd to have to think so far ahead.

This chapter is all about doing some thinking ahead, not about your retirement account, but about what you want your legacy to be. I want to encourage you to think about it to include your work life, but to go beyond work and think about yourself as a whole person. How will you leave your mark? One (morbid-sounding) way to think of it is, at the end of your life, what do you want people to say about you? What is it you hope you leave behind? Senator Paul Tsongas, a US senator from Massachusetts, was diagnosed with a treatable form of cancer. This caused him to reevaluate the direction of his life, and he decided to not seek reelection. He quoted a friend of his who said, "No one on his deathbed ever said, 'I wish I had spent more time at work.'"[30]

What is Higher Purpose?

This legacy you leave should be driven by a sense of what I call your higher purpose. This involves thinking beyond just your job or financial goals. What is the mark you want to leave on Earth? How do you want to impact the people in your life? What is the difference you want to make? Over time you will find that being clear on your higher purpose can serve as a lens to look through when you need to make tough decisions.

When I went through the life-changing Betsy Magness Leadership Program, one of the sessions encouraged us to think about our higher purpose. I will always remember what Elaine Yarbrough, one of the facilitators, said, "There are two things that people think about on their death bed. Who have I loved, and who has loved me?" After the moving session, I continued the conversation with Elaine, whose company, The Yarbrough Group, "helps develops the human side of organizations to ignite the genius of systems, teams, and people." It was at that moment that my higher purpose began to crystallize in my own head.

I mentioned in the last chapter that writing this book is a way for me to pay it forward. I also believe it supports my higher purpose, which is to give back from my cumulative experience and knowledge to help others. In particular, I hope to be helpful to aspiring young people (and especially young women) at the beginning of their careers. I love coaching and mentoring and have done a lot of it over my career. This book is a way for me to reach and impact even more people. I know what it means to have someone support me every step of the way, and it is my hope to help others.

But my higher purpose isn't just about work. My family is always my priority, and a big part of my—and Joel's—higher purpose has always been to parent in a way that creates three well-rounded, healthy, happy adults, who pass that on to their current and future families. When I think about it, I see how my higher purpose plays out in both places. I want to do everything I can to offer my experience and insights to help others be the best people they can be.

Joel's Take

Once you identify your higher purpose, it transforms you into a person who is focused beyond the day-to-day. It is so easy, under the weight of work and family responsibilities, to have a self-centered focus. Higher purpose is something that gives people a reason for being beyond yourself. Your higher purpose can help you leave the world better than you found it.

I've always seen my special purpose as helping people wherever possible just have a little better life and be a little bit happier. I want them to know that, with me, they have a friend who cares about them. I try to do this every day, and sometimes I'm successful and other times I'm not. I recently got a text from a guy asking me what's up. He was a former barista at the Starbucks I went to on most days. Over time I got to know him a little bit and learned that he was an aspiring rapper who was building a music career. The more I got to know him, the more I learned that he wrote thought-provoking lyrics and had unique rapping skills. I know this because he invited me to one his shows. I think he was surprised when I showed up (way past my bedtime by the way). And, as most people in the entertainment world do, he was struggling starting out. I ended up loaning him $100 so that he could buy a piece of audio equipment he needed. He paid me back a couple weeks later.

I would like to say that my involvement rocketed him to stardom. (He is, after all, an internationally known rapper these days, and has done well for himself.) That's not the case. He got where he is today through his hard work and focus. And my higher purpose isn't to create star entertainers, it is to help somebody be a little bit happier. But you never know how that can turn out for the better. He seems like the kind of guy who will remember this and, as Phyllis points out in the previous chapter, pay it forward.

That is a fun story to tell, but most of living out my higher purpose is on a smaller scale. It involves thanking the busboy for cleaning our table at the diner, asking a stranger who might be struggling if they need help loading their car at the supermarket, or just calling someone to check in on them. I have found there are almost no limits to finding ways to make people's lives just a fraction better. And I truly believe that my rapper friend would be the first person to pay it forward by lending someone else a few bucks if he thought he could help them. After all, that's how paying it forward works.

This Idea Will Grow on You

You're probably thinking, "Wait a minute. You're telling me that I have to make another long-term life decision right now—on top of all the other decisions I have been making? I just finished a bunch of important decisions. What do I major in? Where do I want to live when I graduate? What kind of job should I try for? How can I be successful in my first job—or second? And now I am supposed to figure out my higher purpose?"

I'm not pretending that discovering your higher purpose is easy. No lightning bolt of clarity and self-awareness is going to come down from the sky to strike you. It is a matter of paying attention to your own values and seeing how those begin to play out over time. What fulfills you? What makes you feel worthwhile? When you are having a terrific day, what is going on? Just like your retirement savings plan, the sooner you figure it out, the more return you gain from it.

My own higher purpose evolved over time. It started to develop when I began to manage teams and find ways to help my team members grow. At first it was fairly informal, but it became more formalized at Turner Broadcasting when I co-founded a female resource group called Turner Women Today (which still exists). It snowballed from there. Through the years I followed my higher purpose by creating mentoring and leadership development programs and becoming a certified professional coach.

What I didn't expect was how doing this work for others would immensely enrich my own life. Living my higher purpose motivates me to be a better person, to see the good in others, to look at the glass half full, and to be grateful every day for my blessings.

My Higher Purpose and Coaching Others

In my coaching work today, I strive to help others become their best selves. As I explained earlier, coaches do not provide the answers but instead encourage their clients to forge their own path and future. My job as a coach may be to hold you accountable, cheer you on, and/or help you explore challenges and possible solutions.

I believe that when women rise to powerful positions, they can enrich their own lives, shape the success of their companies, and make the world a better place for others. I also know from experience that the first few years of your career are the launch pad for your future success. By following some of the tactics I have described in this book, you will position yourself to rocket every bit of your potential as well as help others to do the same.

Enjoy the journey, and good luck!

Chapter Countdown

MAIN TAKEAWAYS FROM THIS CHAPTER:

- Thinking about your higher purpose requires you to think into the future.
- Spend time considering the mark you want to leave on the world.
- Your higher purpose should transcend your job role.
- Getting clarity on your higher purpose may take some time.
- Your higher purpose will serve as a rudder when you must make tough decisions.

Endnotes

1   Webster's Ninth New Collegiate Dictionary 1021. 1988.

2   Adeno Addis. "Role Models and the Politics of Recognition." *University of Pennsylvania Law Review*, 1996.

3   Gotian, Ruth. "Why You Need a Role Model, Mentor, Coach and Sponsor." Forbes.com, August 4, 2020. https://www.forbes.com/sites/ruthgotian/?sh=35b86cdff7de

4   McCall, Morgan W. Jr, Lombardo, Michael, and Morrison, Ann M. *The Lessons of Experience: How Successful Executives Develop on the Job*. New York: Lexington Books, 1988.

5   Levy, John. *You're Invited: The Art and Science of Cultivating Influence*. New York: Harper Business, 2021.

6   Chui, Michael, Manyika, James, Bughin, Jacques, Dobbs, Richard, Roxburgh, Charles, Sarrazin, Hugo, Sands, Geoffrey, and Westergren, Magdalena. "The social economy: Unlocking value and productivity through social technologies." *McKinsey Global Institute Report*. July 1, 2012. https://www.mckinsey.com/industries/technology-media-and-telecommunications/our-insights/the-social-economy

7   Gordon, Amie M. "Do Gratitude Journals Really Work?" *Psychology Today*, March 15, 2019. https://www.psychologytoday.com/us/blog/between-you-and-me/201903/do-gratitude-journals-really-work-4-new-gratitude-findings.

8   "Giving thanks can make you happier." *Harvard Health Publishing*, August 14, 2021. https://www.health.harvard.edu/healthbeat/giving-thanks-can-make-you-happier.

9   Poague, Emily. "These are the 6 skills college grads need to compete in the post-Covid jobs market." CNBC At Work Newsletter. LinkedIn June 4, 2020. https://www.cnbc.com/2020/06/02/linkedin-6-skills-college-grads-need-to-land-post-coronavirus-jobs.html.

10   Abel, Jaison R. and Deitz, Richard. "Agglomeration and Job Matching among College Graduates." Federal Reserve Bank of New York. Staff Report No. 587. December 2012, rev. December 2014. https://www.newyorkfed.org/research/staff_reports/sr587.html.

11   Post, Stephen G. "It's good to be good: 2011 fifth annual scientific report on health, happiness and helping others." *International Journal of Person-Centered Medicine*, December 20, 2011.

12   Tinsley, Catherine H. and Ely, Robin J. "What Most People Get Wrong About Men and Women." *Harvard Business Review*, May–June 2018.

13   kpCompanies. "How to Manage a Multi-Generational Workforce." September 7, 2020. https://kpcompanies.com/how-to-manage-a-multi-generational-workforce/.

14   Zempke, Ron, Raines, Claire, and Filipczak, Bob. "Generations at Work: Managing the Clash of Veterans, Boomers, Xers, and Nexters in Your Workplace." New York: American Management Association, 2000.

15   King, Eden, Finkelstein, Lisa, Thomas, Courtney, and Corrington, Abby. "Generational Differences at Work are Small. Thinking They're Big Affects our Behavior." HBR.org, August 1, 2019. https://hbr.org/2019/08/generational-differences-at-work-are-small-thinking-theyre-big-affects-our-behavior.

16 Burns, Tiffany, Huang, Jess, Krivkovich, Alexis, Rambachan, Ishanaa, Trkulja, Tijana, and Yee, Lareina. "Women in the Workplace 2021." McKinsey & Company, September 27, 2021. https://www.mckinsey.com/featured-insights/diversity-and-inclusion/women-in-the-workplace.

17 Ibid.

18 Schwartz, Barry. *The paradox of choice: Why more Is Less.* New York: Harper Perennial, 2004.

19 Schwartz, Barry. "The paradox of choice." Ted Talk at TEDGlobal 2005. https://www.ted.com/talks/barry_schwartz_the_paradox_of_choice?language=en.

20 Rutledge, Robb. "Would you be happier if you lowered your expectations?" Psychology Today Blog. June 2, 2021. https://www.psychologytoday.com/us/blog/the-happiness-equation/202106/would-you-be-happier-if-you-lowered-your-expectations.

21 Deutschman, Alan. "Change or die." Fast Company Blog, May 1, 2005. https://www.fastcompany.com/52717/change-or-die.

22 Onken, William and Wass, Donald L. "Management time: who's got the monkey?" *Harvard Business Review*, November–December 1999. https://hbr.org/1999/11/management-time-whos-got-the-monkey.

23 Sandberg, S. and Scovell, Nell. *Lean In: Women, Work, and the Will to Lead.* New York: Alfred A. Knopf, 2013.

24 LinkedIn. "Global talent trends 2020." https://business.linkedin.com/talent-solutions/recruiting-tips/global-talent-trends-2020.

25 Gallo, Mary. "Setting the Record Straight on Switching Jobs." *Harvard Business Review*, October 2015. https://hbr.org/2015/07/setting-the-record-straight-on-switching-jobs.

26   Bureau of Labor Statistics news release. "Employee tenure in 2020." USDL-20-1791 September 22, 2020. https://www.bls.gov/news.release/pdf/tenure.pdf.

27   Mathews, Ian. "How Long Should I Stay If I Took the Wrong Job?" Forbes.com, June 26, 2019. https://www.forbes.com/sites/ianmathews/2019/06/26/how-long-should-i-stay-if-i-took-the-wrong-job/?sh=3251abdb1878.

28   Oman, Doug. "Does volunteering foster physical health and longevity?" In S.G. Post (Ed.), *Altruism and health: Perspectives from empirical research*. Oxford University Press, 2003.

29   Tsvetkova, Milena and Macy, Michael. "The Science of 'Paying It Forward.'" Nytimes.com, March 14, 2014. https://www.nytimes.com/2014/03/16/opinion/sunday/the-science-of-paying-it-forward.html.

30   Tsongas, Paul. *Heading Home*. New York: Alfred A. Knopf, 1984.

About the Author

Phyllis Ehrlich ignites business, transforms teams, champions rising talent, and inspires future women leaders. Beginning in the publishing industry, Phyllis rose to executive roles with the Walt Disney Company, Turner Broadcasting, and Time Warner. She is currently Group Vice President at Charter Communications/Spectrum Reach, leading the Client Success team.

Phyllis is an alumna of The WICT Network's Betsy Magness Leadership Institute, Stanford Business School Senior Executive Summit, and the Cable Executive Management Program at Harvard Business School.

Phyllis' passion is helping working women hone their skills to reach their career potential and achieve their long-term goals. With her expertise in women's early career professional development and high-energy presentation style, she is in demand as a speaker, coach, and consultant.

As a Certified Professional Coach by the Institute for Excellence in Coaching, Phylls excels at helping others unlock their career potential.

Phyllis and her husband, Joel, share a love of theater and the arts. She is the proud mom/stepmom to Andrew, Jennifer and Jonathan. Phyllis is an avid fitness enthusiast and continues on her quest to rocket her own struggling golf game.

You can contact her at Phyllis.Ehrlich@gmail.com or LinkedIn (https://www.linkedin.com/in/phyllisehrlich/).